I0461572

# The Manifest Principles in Business

## How Energy, Alignment and Conscious Leadership Create Extraordinary Companies

Christine Zanjanipour

**DETAILS MATTER BOOKS**

ISBN: **979-8-9939013-0-5**
First Edition

Published by Details Matter Books

Printed in the United States of America

For more information, visit:
[www.DetailsMatterBooks.com]

To my mom —

for showing me, every single day, that mindset shapes reality.

For reminding me, since I was a little girl,

that I could become anything I dreamed of being.


. I Love You So Very Much.

# Table of Contents

# Introduction

Energy doesn't follow strategy — strategy follows energy. This book was born in the quiet moments between meetings, deadlines, and flights — in that sacred space where the noise of business fades just long enough for you to hear something deeper.

I didn't set out to write a book about business. I set out to understand why some companies flourish with ease while others grind endlessly without ever feeling fulfilled. I wanted to know why two leaders could have the same resources, the same market, the same strategy — and yet one moves with magnetic flow while the other fights resistance every step of the way.

Over time, I found my answer.
It wasn't in spreadsheets or software.
It wasn't in meetings or marketing plans.
It was in **energy.**

The companies that thrive — the ones that seem to attract opportunity effortlessly — operate at a higher vibration. Their leaders are clear. Their culture is emotionally aligned. Their people feel connected to something meaningful.

What I discovered is this:

Energy is the true infrastructure of every successful business.

## The Spark

I've spent decades working in the homebuilding industry, leading teams, developing partnerships, and driving growth for incredible companies. I've watched brands rise, evolve, and reinvent themselves.

I've seen the tension between creativity and control, intuition and data, soul and structure.

And somewhere along the way, I realized — business wasn't separate from the energy I was studying in my personal life.
The same Manifest Principles that shaped how I live — **Clarity, Belief, Emotional Alignment, Inspired Action, Detachment, Identity Alignment and Overcoming Resistance** — were quietly shaping every success story I witnessed in leadership.

When teams were clear, aligned, and emotionally coherent, results came easily.
When energy was low or leadership was reactive, growth felt impossible.

The difference wasn't strategy.
It was **state of being.**

## The Shift

The deeper I went into this work, the more obvious it became: Business is a mirror. It reflects the energy of its leaders, its culture, its intention. You can't build an abundant company from scarcity. You can't lead with clarity if you operate in fear. And you can't manifest flow when you're gripping control.

So what if we stopped trying to separate the spiritual from the practical? What if leadership could feel both intentional and intuitive? What if profit could coexist with peace?

That's what this book explores — the meeting point between **conscious energy and effective leadership.**

When you integrate these Manifest Principles into business, you begin to see how alignment is strategy, how trust becomes structure, and how presence itself becomes performance.

The vibration of your company is the sum of the energy within it.

## The Invitation

This isn't a business manual. It's a recalibration.
It's an invitation to remember that behind every product, project, and profit statement is energy — your energy, your team's energy, your company's collective frequency.

Each chapter offers both reflection and practice — ideas to awaken alignment, real-world stories of transformation, and practical ways to bring energy into everyday operations.

You'll see how culture begins with clarity, how communication shapes vibration, how detachment creates flow, and how receiving becomes a form of leadership.

You'll also see how resistance, doubt, and fear aren't signs of failure — they're signals for alignment. They're opportunities to lead differently.

My hope is that as you move through these pages, you don't just learn — you feel. You'll begin to notice where your business feels light and alive, and where it feels heavy and forced.
And with that awareness, you'll begin to shift from effort to energy, from control to co-creation.

## The Promise

This book is for the leaders who are ready to do business differently — the ones who know that culture isn't a campaign, it's a vibration.
That success isn't just about growth, it's about resonance.
And that every goal, every milestone, every innovation begins with energy.

If you've ever felt that your work was meant to mean more — this is your reminder that it can.
If you've ever felt that leadership could be more intuitive, more human, more aligned — it can.

3

And if you've ever wondered how to bring spirituality into strategy without losing credibility — this is your bridge.

Because business and consciousness are not opposites.
They are two sides of the same creation.

My wish is that these principles guide you, ground you, and gently transform the way you build, lead, and believe. That as you embody them, your company — and everyone in it — becomes a living expression of alignment.

And that as you lead, you remember this truth:

You are not just running a business.
You are shaping energy.
And when energy aligns — success becomes inevitable.

# Manifesto: The Energy of Conscious Business

We believe business is energy in motion.

Every idea, every meeting, every decision carries a vibration.
Every person in a company is a frequency.
Every culture is a collective field of intention.

We believe that profit and purpose are not opposites.
They are partners — born of the same current.
When energy flows freely through an organization, abundance follows naturally.

We believe leadership is energetic stewardship.
A conscious leader doesn't push — they align.
They don't manage people — they harmonize energy.
They don't chase growth — they become it.

We believe that clarity creates direction.
Belief creates momentum.
Emotion creates connection.
And alignment creates everything.

We believe success is not built through pressure, but through presence.
Not through competition, but through coherence.
Not through control, but through trust.

We believe culture is not what's written on the wall — it's what's felt in the room.
It's the tone of the email, the energy of the meeting, the pause before the response.
It's the invisible that creates the visible.

We believe that business is not separate from consciousness —
it is consciousness, organized into action.

We believe the future of leadership belongs to those who can feel energy as clearly as they can read a spreadsheet.
To those who know that the unseen drives the seen,
and that the vibration of one aligned team can move mountains.

We believe that resistance is simply energy asking to move.
That chaos is clarity in disguise.
That alignment is always available.

We believe that when we raise the vibration of business,
we raise the vibration of the world.

Because every client interaction is an exchange of frequency.
Every brand message is a transmission.
Every moment of integrity strengthens the field of possibility.

And every conscious company —
every leader who chooses alignment over ego, energy over effort,
belief over fear —
is quietly changing the collective.

This is what we build.
This is what we lead.
This is what we manifest.

We are the new architecture of business —
energy-built, heart-led, and universally aligned.

An d above all, **We speak clearly, act consciously, and lead intentionally —because the Universe is always listening**

# The New Currency of Leadership

For decades, we've measured leadership by metrics — performance, output, efficiency, revenue. But the leaders of this new era know something deeper: those numbers are not the source of power. They are the reflection of it. The new currency of leadership isn't control. It isn't even confidence. It's energy.

Your energy — your clarity, your alignment, your belief — determines everything. It shapes how your team feels in your presence. It colors the tone of your meetings. It sets the vibration for your company culture before a single strategy ever takes form.

In this modern landscape, where employees crave meaning and connection as much as stability, leaders who can manage energy — not just operations — are the ones who thrive. They understand that alignment creates momentum, that emotional coherence breeds innovation, and that belief is more contagious than fear.

When you walk into a room aligned, people feel it.
They can't always name it, but they sense it. They trust you more, follow more easily, and bring their highest selves forward — not because you demanded it, but because you embodied it.

This is what I call energetic leadership — the ability to create results through resonance instead of resistance. It's leading from presence rather than pressure. It's knowing that your vibration sets the tone for everyone around you.

The leaders who thrive in this new economy are those who are attuned to energy as much as they are to data.
They listen not only to what's being said, but to the frequency underneath it — the emotional truth of their teams and their customers. They lead with empathy, clarity, and intuition,

understanding that business is an energetic ecosystem, not just an operational machine.

When you see business as energy, you stop reacting and start responding. You stop pushing and start aligning. You move from forcing outcomes to allowing them — by holding a clear, unwavering vision and trusting the process.

That's the new currency.
Not time.
Not titles.
Not even money.

The new currency of leadership is energy — because energy creates everything.

As you move forward, remember that energy is not an abstract concept — it's the foundation of every choice, every culture, every result.

The principles that follow are not rules; they are frequencies — the living architecture of alignment in motion.

Each one builds upon the next, guiding you to create a company that breathes with purpose, leads with presence, and manifests with precision.

# Part One

# The 7 Manifest Principles in Business

# Chapter 1 — Clarity: Vision as Energy

"Clarity is not just knowing what you want—it's aligning your energy so everyone around you can see it, feel it, and move toward it."

**Section 1: The Energetics of Clarity**

Every company begins as an idea—a spark, a vision, a conversation that catches light.
But as teams grow, projects multiply, and strategies layer upon strategies, that original spark can blur. People stay busy, calendars filled, reports get longer, and yet something essential goes missing: clarity.

You can feel it when it's gone. Meetings end without decisions. Employees hesitate to act. Projects stall because no one is sure what truly matters. The energy inside the organization becomes scattered— activity without direction, motion without momentum. It's like driving a car with the parking brake half on: there's effort, but no ease.

Contrast that with a company where clarity hums in the air. Everyone, from leadership to entry-level team members, can articulate what the organization stands for and why it exists. The mission isn't a plaque on a wall; it's a pulse that beats through every action. People don't need to be told what to prioritize because they intuitively know what's aligned. Decisions happen faster. Communication feels lighter. Energy flows.

That is the power of clarity.

Clarity is not about knowing every detail of the future. It's about anchoring in a frequency so strong that everyone can find direction within it. It's energetic coherence—the point at which intention and communication align so perfectly that they create movement without force.

When leaders embody clarity, they become tuning forks for the organization. Their steadiness creates harmony; their focus creates trust. Employees no longer operate from confusion or fear of being wrong. Instead, they feel safe to contribute, confident that their work matters.

The truth is, people crave clarity more than they crave certainty. Certainty demands that we know everything. Clarity simply asks that we know what matters most.
In a world of constant noise and rapid change, clarity is the quiet force that keeps an organization in alignment. It doesn't eliminate chaos—it organizes energy around purpose.

Think of clarity as light. When light diffuses, it illuminates gently but lacks focus. When you concentrate it—like a laser—it can cut through steel. The same principle applies to teams. Diffused energy glows. Focused energy transforms.

A leader's first job, then, is not to inspire or to manage, but to clarify. What are we here to create? Why does it matter? And how will we know when we've arrived?

When those questions are answered with heart and precision, the organization begins to self-organize around them. Departments communicate more fluidly. Innovation happens naturally because everyone's creativity points in the same direction. Momentum becomes less about pushing and more about allowing—because the energy is flowing in one clear, unified stream.

Clarity, at its essence, is the first act of manifestation. Before a vision becomes strategy or a goal becomes reality, it must first exist as a clear, unconfused thought—an intention free of energetic noise.
For individuals, that clarity defines purpose. For companies, it defines culture.

Clarity is the starting point for everything that follows in this book. It's the foundation upon which belief, emotion, action, and identity are built. Without it, even the most passionate teams lose their way. With it, even the most complex organizations can move as one.

So, as we explore the principles of manifestation in business, remember this: clarity isn't something you find. It's something you create—and then continually recalibrate as your organization evolves.

Because when clarity exists, energy aligns. And when energy aligns, manifestation begins.

## Section 2: Vision Clarity — The Corporate North Star

Every organization has a vision statement.
Few, however, have a vision frequency.

A vision statement is words on a website — something people can quote but not necessarily feel.
A vision frequency is an energy that guides behavior, conversation, and decision-making. It's what happens when a company's purpose is so clear, so alive, that everyone can sense whether an idea or action is aligned with it.

True clarity of vision is not just what a company does, but why it exists. It's not a paragraph written for investors or customers; it's a compass that orients every person within the organization. When vision clarity is strong, people no longer need to check in for approval on every step — they can sense what's right because they understand the "why" beneath the "what."

Think of companies whose teams move with ease and unity. It's not that they have fewer challenges; it's that they have direction. They know what hill they're climbing and why it matters. Their daily actions—emails, meetings, product choices—are infused with that clarity. There's an energetic hum that you can almost hear when people believe in what they're building.

Vision clarity answers three questions with precision and feeling:

1. **Who are we?**
2. **What are we here to create?**
3. **Why does it matter?**

When those three questions are answered with energy instead of jargon, people connect. They begin to see the same picture in their minds. That is alignment — not everyone thinking alike, but everyone thinking in the same direction.

## The Vision Audit

Clarity begins with honesty.
Every leadership team should pause and ask:

1. Can every employee describe the company's purpose in one clear sentence?
2. Do leaders communicate the same message consistently across departments?
3. Are our goals, investments, and initiatives directly aligned with that vision?
4. Are we measuring success based on what we truly value, or just what's easy to track?

If any of those answers feel fuzzy, clarity has begun to fade — not because the company lacks ambition, but because the energetic signal has weakened. The good news? It can be restored quickly through awareness and alignment.

One CEO I once interviewed said, "When we stopped using the phrase 'maximize shareholder value' and started saying, 'We make life simpler for small business owners,' everything changed."

That single act of clarity reoriented the entire company. Employees began to innovate around simplicity. Customer service improved. Meetings shortened. The purpose was no longer abstract — it was embodied.

Vision clarity is contagious. When leadership speaks it, people remember it. When they embody it, people repeat it. When it's consistent, it becomes culture.

**The Power of Precision**

A clear vision doesn't require long explanations. It needs resonance. It should be felt as much as understood.

Consider this difference:

- "Our mission is to leverage digital platforms to enhance customer engagement."
  vs.
- "We help people feel seen."

Both could describe the same company. But only one speaks to the heart — and hearts are what move organizations forward.

Clarity brings simplicity. Simplicity brings power. Power creates alignment.
And alignment is what turns words into momentum.

**Energetic Alignment Checkpoint**

- Does our vision statement create emotion or obligation?

- When we read it aloud, does it feel true, or does it feel safe?

- Can every team member connect their daily work to this vision?

If the answers are yes, your company is moving in alignment.
If not, clarity is calling you to refine the message — not to start over, but to speak truth in a way that reignites collective belief.

Because a company without clarity is like a ship without a compass. It can still move, but it will drift endlessly, expending energy without ever reaching its destination.

Vision clarity doesn't tell people what to do; it reminds them why it matters.

And when everyone remembers why, energy naturally follows how.

When the destination is clear, decisions become simple.

## Section 3: Communication Clarity — The Language of Alignment

If vision is the North Star, communication is the light that reflects it. Clarity may begin in the boardroom, but it either lives or dies in conversation.

Every organization runs on language. Memos, emails, presentations, meetings — they're the invisible architecture of how energy moves. Yet in many companies, that language becomes tangled in jargon, acronyms, and half-hearted phrases. People talk in circles, decisions blur, and alignment begins to fracture.

When communication lacks clarity, energy leaks everywhere. Leaders repeat themselves. Employees interpret messages differently. Teams lose momentum because they're all walking in the same direction with slightly different maps.

You can feel this confusion energetically. It sounds like defensiveness in meetings, silence in brainstorms, or the subtle heaviness that follows every "urgent update." The company may look productive, but the vibration feels scattered. People are working hard — but not necessarily in harmony.

## The Frequency of Words

Words are energy carriers.
They don't just describe reality — they create it.

When leaders speak with conviction, tone, and simplicity, their words transmit confidence. When they use vague or overly polished language, it sends a different frequency — one of distance or doubt.

The most powerful communication is not grand; it's grounded. It says just enough for people to understand, remember, and act. It feels human, not rehearsed.

Because people don't follow PowerPoint slides — they follow energy. They align with leaders who make them feel safe, inspired, and seen.

## The Three C's of Clarity

To restore alignment through communication, practice the Three C's:

1. **Consistency** — Say the same thing everywhere. Consistency creates trust. Every meeting, message, and update should reinforce the same essence of vision.

2. **Conciseness** — Speak simply. Replace "leverage," "synergize," and "vertical integration" with words that your grandmother would understand. Simplicity is not unsophisticated — it's magnetic.

3. **Candor** — Be direct. Say what you mean. Authenticity clears static faster than any rebrand ever could.

If you can communicate a message so clearly that it could be repeated by anyone in your organization, you've achieved energetic clarity.

**Exercise: "Message in a Minute"**

Invite your leadership team to share your company's vision out loud — but they each have only 60 seconds to do it.

- No notes.
- No buzzwords.
- No corporate language.
  Just heart and truth.

You'll learn quickly where clarity has become diluted. Some will speak from the mind; others from the heart. Both matter, but the magic lies in merging the two — clear thought, spoken with authentic energy.

When people speak from alignment, others feel it. The words vibrate with integrity. They don't just communicate direction; they transmit belief.

**Energetic Integrity in Communication**

Clarity in communication isn't only about words — it's about energy matching message.
You can say all the right things, but if your tone carries impatience or fear, people will pick up that frequency first.
Energy precedes language.

If you want your company's communication to inspire trust, you must first embody it.

Ask yourself:

- Do I speak from anxiety or from calm authority?

- Do I rush through communication or allow space for understanding?

- Do I repeat the message often enough that it becomes culture?

When communication is clear, energy flows. When communication is cluttered, energy stagnates.

Leadership communication, then, is not a performance; it's a practice — a daily choice to speak truth in simple, energetic alignment with the company's purpose.

Every email, meeting, and memo either adds to clarity or confusion. Choose consciously.

## Section 4: Strategic Clarity — From Vision to Execution

Vision without direction is poetry.
Direction without vision is exhaustion.
Strategic clarity is where the two meet — where inspired purpose becomes focused movement.

Most organizations don't fail because they lack ideas. They fail because they lack focus. When every initiative feels equally important, nothing truly moves forward. The company's energy becomes diluted — lots of motion, little momentum.

Strategic clarity isn't about having the perfect plan; it's about knowing which few things will move the needle and aligning every ounce of energy behind them.

A clear strategy feels like a current. Everyone can sense the flow. You don't need to push people downstream when the direction is obvious — they move naturally with it.

## The Cost of Confusion

When strategy isn't clear, organizations start compensating with busyness.
Meetings multiply. Reports grow longer. Teams create complexity in an unconscious attempt to justify effort. But all of that activity masks the truth: confusion at the top always becomes chaos at the bottom.

Lack of clarity is expensive. It drains time, morale, and trust.
Employees begin to hesitate — they fear misalignment or wasted work. Managers overcorrect with control. Innovation slows, not because people lack creativity, but because they lack confidence in direction.

You can measure this loss of clarity by the number of competing priorities in your company.
If everything is a priority, nothing is.

## The Energy Leak Inventory

To restore strategic clarity, leaders must first locate the leaks — those projects, meetings, or habits that consume energy without contributing meaningfully to the vision.

Ask yourself:

- Which initiatives have lost their momentum but remain out of habit?

- Where are we saying "yes" when we should be saying "not now"?

- What tasks drain enthusiasm but deliver little value?

The act of clarifying strategy often begins not with adding, but with releasing.
When you consciously remove what no longer serves the mission, the

organization breathes again. People regain energy because focus returns.

One global company once realized that nearly 30% of its projects didn't directly support its stated goals. When they courageously cut them, employees reported less burnout and greater engagement. Clarity creates efficiency — not through pressure, but through alignment.

## From Vision to Action

Strategic clarity requires translating the "why" into measurable "how." It's the bridge that connects inspiration to execution.

Here's a simple framework that every leadership team can adopt:

1. **Define the Core Vision** — What are we here to achieve this year that aligns with our purpose?

2. **Name Three Strategic Anchors** — What three priorities matter most right now?

3. **Establish Aligned Metrics** — How will we know we're succeeding, not just performing?

4. **Communicate the Flow** — How does each department contribute to this shared direction?

When every level of the organization understands not only what to do, but why it matters, the atmosphere changes. Meetings become more decisive. Employees start thinking proactively rather than reactively. Leaders spend less time managing and more time mentoring.

## Simplify to Amplify

Great leaders are editors, not accumulators.
They continually refine, simplify, and distill the company's efforts into what matters most.

Simplicity is not the absence of ambition; it's the amplification of impact.
When people know exactly what to focus on, energy compounds. Every action reinforces the next.

Strategic clarity transforms "busy" into "effective."
It invites teams to move from reaction to intention — from scattered motion to focused creation.

Focus is the most underestimated leadership tool.

## Section 5: The Energetic Benefits of Clarity

Clarity is often viewed as a leadership skill, but it's far more than that — it's a form of energetic hygiene.
It keeps the company's vibration clean, coherent, and strong. When clarity exists, tension eases, creativity expands, and people naturally align without the need for constant supervision or motivation.

You can feel the difference between a clear company and a cloudy one. In clear environments, conversations flow easily. Questions are welcomed. The "why" behind decisions is known. Even when challenges arise, people respond rather than react. The energy feels calm yet alive — confident yet adaptable.

In unclear organizations, the opposite happens.
Meetings feel heavy. Every announcement is met with confusion or skepticism. Employees expend emotional energy trying to interpret what leaders actually mean. This lack of clarity creates friction — a subtle drag that slows everything down.

The human body offers the perfect analogy. When energy in the body flows freely, there's health and vitality. When the system is blocked or congested, fatigue and imbalance appear. A company's energy works the same way: clarity keeps the channels open so that creativity, trust, and action can move unimpeded.

## Clarity Reduces Anxiety

Uncertainty breeds fear.
When people don't know what's expected or why something is happening, their nervous systems activate protective behaviors: hesitation, withdrawal, defensiveness. They cling to what's familiar because the unknown feels unsafe.

Clarity is an antidote to that fear. It restores safety through understanding.
When leaders communicate clearly — even about difficult topics like restructuring or shifting priorities — people can process and adapt. They may not love the change, but they trust it. That trust becomes stability, and stability is the foundation of innovation.

When employees feel grounded, they spend less energy managing emotion and more energy creating. That's why clarity isn't just kind — it's efficient. It saves emotional bandwidth across the organization.

## Clarity Fuels Confidence

People crave certainty about their role in the vision. They want to know that what they do matters.
When leaders articulate how each person's contribution connects to the bigger purpose, a spark ignites. Employees move from compliance to commitment. They stop doing the bare minimum and start thinking, "What else is possible?"

Clarity gives people permission to act boldly because they understand the boundaries of alignment. It's not control — it's empowerment through direction.

Imagine a team of musicians. Without a conductor, even talented players can sound dissonant. But when the tempo, key, and intention are clear, they don't need to watch every move — they feel the rhythm together. That's what clarity does in a company: it creates rhythm.

## Clarity Strengthens Trust

Trust and clarity are inseparable.
When people know where the company is headed and why, they relax into their roles. They trust leadership's decisions because they can see the logic and integrity behind them. They also trust one another more, because there's less competition for attention or approval.

In many ways, clarity is the highest form of respect. It says: "I value you enough to be honest with you." It eliminates unnecessary politics and gossip because communication is direct. Transparency becomes a cultural norm, not an occasional act of courage.

When a company runs on clarity, it feels peaceful even in growth. There's movement, but not chaos. Ambition, but not anxiety. People are busy, but they're not burned out. They're engaged because they understand how their energy contributes to the whole.

## The Science of Clarity

Neuroscience supports what energy leaders have long known: the human brain craves clear signals. When direction is vague, the amygdala — the brain's threat detector — activates, producing stress hormones like cortisol.
When direction is clear, the prefrontal cortex takes over, opening access to creativity, problem-solving, and empathy.

Clarity literally changes the chemistry of your organization. It shifts people from survival mode to creation mode.

So while many leaders chase strategy, innovation, and performance metrics, the most effective leaders start with clarity — because everything else becomes easier from there.

When clarity is present, people flourish.
When it's absent, even the best intentions unravel.

Clarity is not just communication — it's calm. It's trust. It's freedom.

## Section 6: Manifest This in Your Company — Exercises

Clarity isn't built in a meeting or a memo — it's built in practice.
It deepens through reflection, conversation, and repetition until it becomes cultural muscle memory.
The following exercises are designed to help leadership teams, managers, and employees not only define clarity, but embody it.

### 1. Vision Audit Workshop

**Purpose:** To assess how clearly the organization's purpose and direction are understood throughout all levels.

**How to do it:**

- Gather a cross-section of employees (different departments, roles, and tenures).

- Ask everyone to write their answer to three questions:

  1. What is our company's vision?

  2. Why does it matter?

  3. How does your role contribute to it?

- Compare the answers.

**The insight:**
If you see diverse interpretations, it doesn't mean failure — it means opportunity. Misalignment isn't personal; it's energetic feedback. Leadership can then refine the vision statement until the energy of it feels both true and simple enough to be repeated by everyone.

Clarity isn't consensus; it's coherence.

### 2. The Clarity Statement Rewrite

**Purpose:** To distill your company's mission or vision into one emotionally resonant sentence.

**How to do it:**

- Write your existing mission statement on a board.
- Ask: "If this sentence had a heartbeat, what would it feel like?"
- Rewrite it in language a customer or child could understand.
- Remove every buzzword until what remains feels human and real.
- Test it aloud — if it doesn't create an emotional response, keep refining.

**Example:**

- Before: "We leverage technology to optimize human connection across platforms."
- After: "We help people stay close, no matter where they are."

Clarity lives in simplicity. The truer the statement, the stronger the energy.

### 3. The Energy Alignment Meeting

**Purpose:** To ensure projects, goals, and decisions remain aligned with the company's vision.

**How to do it:**
Once a month, hold a short leadership session called an Energy Alignment Meeting.

- Begin by reading the company vision aloud.
- Review major initiatives.

- Ask: "Does this project amplify our vision or distract from it?"
- If it amplifies, invest more energy. If it distracts, refine or release it.

When teams pause regularly to realign, they protect their most precious resource: collective energy.

## 4. The Clarity Pulse Check

**Purpose:** To create ongoing awareness of how clear communication and direction feel across the organization.

**How to do it:**
Send out a quarterly, two-question anonymous survey:

1. Do you feel clear on where our company is headed?
2. Do you feel clear on how your work contributes to that direction?

Track responses over time.
When clarity drops, don't panic — get curious. Ask what changed: leadership messaging, team structure, or external noise? Each data point becomes an opportunity to re-center communication and renew energy alignment.

## 5. The One-Page Plan

**Purpose:** To translate clarity into strategy that everyone can see and remember.

**How to do it:**

- On a single page, summarize your vision, top three priorities, and measures of success.
- Distribute it to every employee.

- Encourage teams to post it visually in workspaces.

Clarity thrives when it's visible.
When people can literally see the path forward, they stop questioning direction and start manifesting results.

## 6. The 5-Minute Clarity Reset

**Purpose:** To bring clarity into personal leadership moments.

Whenever you feel overwhelmed, try this:

- Step away from your desk.

- Close your eyes.

- Ask yourself: "What actually matters right now?"

- Choose one next aligned action — not five.

This micro-practice helps leaders operate from grounded intention rather than reaction.
Over time, it creates a culture where calm focus replaces chronic busyness.

### Energetic Takeaway

Clarity doesn't come from effort — it comes from alignment.
When you practice returning to the core message, the noise fades.
The path doesn't have to be perfectly mapped; it just has to be clear enough to walk.

Manifestation begins the moment you can articulate your truth with simplicity and belief.

### Section 7: Reflection Prompts

Clarity is both collective and personal.
It begins at the leadership level, but it also lives inside every individual's awareness — in how they think, speak, and choose their actions each day.

These reflection prompts are designed to bring awareness to where clarity flows easily in your organization… and where it may be clouded. Set aside quiet time to reflect alone, or use these prompts to spark conversation in team workshops or one-on-one coaching sessions.

## For Leaders

### 1. Where might I be sending mixed energetic signals?
Do my words and actions match the energy of the vision I've communicated? If not, what needs to realign — my message, my mindset, or my tone?

### 2. What conversations am I avoiding that could create clarity?
Avoidance breeds confusion. Clarity requires courage. Where could transparency, even if uncomfortable, restore trust and direction?

### 3. How can I make the company's vision feel more human?
When people connect emotionally to a purpose, they remember it. How can I speak in a way that touches hearts, not just minds?

### 4. What am I overcomplicating that could be simplified?
True clarity is often found in subtraction — removing extra words, extra steps, or extra noise. What could I eliminate this week to make space for simplicity?

### 5. How does clarity feel energetically in my body?
When I'm clear, do I feel calm? Focused? Expansive? Learn your own energetic cues. Your body often knows when the organization is aligned before your mind does.

## For Teams

### 1. Do I fully understand how my work connects to our larger vision?
If not, what do I need to ask my manager or leadership to feel more grounded in purpose?

### 2. Where do I feel confusion or mixed direction?
Instead of assuming it's "just me," can I raise the question with curiosity and kindness to help the team find alignment?

### 3. How do I communicate with clarity?
Do my emails, meetings, and updates create calm and direction, or do they add noise? How might I simplify my own messages to reflect clarity back into the culture?

### 4. When I don't have clarity, what do I do?
Do I pause, seek understanding, or push ahead from fear? Learning how you handle uncertainty is the first step toward mastering it.

### 5. How does clarity affect my energy?
Notice the difference between days when you know exactly what matters and days when you're unsure. How could you recreate that sense of clarity intentionally each morning?

## Team Reflection Ritual

Try closing a weekly team meeting with this simple question:

"What's one thing we're clear on — and one thing we're not?"

This practice normalizes honesty and keeps communication open. Over time, it becomes a shared energetic reset — a way to maintain alignment before confusion turns into resistance.

Clarity is not a one-time declaration; it's a continual act of remembering.
Every conversation is a chance to choose coherence over confusion, presence over pressure, simplicity over noise.

Clarity doesn't shout. It speaks softly and confidently — and everyone listens.

## Section 8: Closing Affirmation

Clarity is the first breath of every manifestation.
It is the moment when fog becomes form — when vision stops being an idea and starts becoming a frequency the whole organization can feel.

When clarity is present, decisions don't demand effort; they emerge naturally.
Teams move with rhythm instead of resistance.
Leaders speak and the message doesn't echo — it lands.
Energy no longer leaks into confusion, because everyone knows what they are here to create and why it matters.

Clarity quiets the noise.
It replaces overthinking with direction, and anxiety with trust.
It reminds the company who it is, and calls every individual back to purpose.

So as you move forward, breathe in the simplicity of this truth:

**Clarity creates direction. Direction creates momentum. Momentum manifests success.**

When you lead with clarity, you lead with energy that others can organize around.
And in that space of coherence, the impossible begins to move toward you.

# Chapter 2 — Belief: The Culture Multiplier

"A company doesn't become great because people are told to believe in it — it becomes great because they genuinely do."

## Section 1: The Energetics of Belief

Belief is the invisible infrastructure of every successful organization. It's what fills the space between a company's vision and its execution. You can have clarity about where you're going, but belief is what convinces people it's possible to get there.

Walk into any thriving workplace and you'll feel it instantly. There's a pulse of confidence, a quiet certainty in the air. People move quickly but not anxiously. Decisions don't linger in endless debate. Teams celebrate small wins because they trust they're building toward something real. That's belief made tangible — not hope, but conviction.

Now walk into a struggling organization. You'll sense the opposite frequency: doubt. Ideas are met with hesitation. Projects stall in review cycles. Leaders sound persuasive but not persuasive enough. It's not that people disagree; it's that they no longer believe. The company's words have outpaced its energy.

Belief, like electricity, must stay connected to its source.
When leaders stop radiating genuine conviction, the current weakens. Employees may keep working out of obligation, but their creativity dims. They begin to protect themselves from disappointment. Innovation flat-lines, and culture quietly loses its spark.

## Belief vs. Blind Optimism

Belief isn't pretending everything is perfect.
It's the courage to stay rooted in possibility even when the path is uncertain.

Blind optimism denies problems; belief confronts them with faith in a positive outcome.

In a practical sense, belief is the emotional permission to keep going. It's what enables a team to move through setbacks without collapsing into blame.
It's what transforms failure from evidence of defeat into evidence of progress.

The energetic truth is simple:

- **Clarity** sets direction.
- **Belief** supplies fuel.

One without the other is imbalance. Clarity without belief is a beautiful plan that no one follows. Belief without clarity is enthusiasm without aim. But together, they create alignment — the state where intention, emotion, and action move as one.

**The Resonance Effect**

Belief multiplies because emotion is contagious.
When a leader truly believes, their tone, body language, and decisions transmit confidence. People pick up that frequency subconsciously. They start thinking, If they believe, maybe I can too.

That's how collective belief begins: one steady vibration amplified through trust.
In energetic terms, belief is coherence in motion — individuals aligning to a shared signal. When enough people hold that frequency, the organization becomes magnetic. It attracts talent, opportunities, and partners who resonate with the same energy.

The opposite is also true. Doubt creates dissonance. When disbelief spreads, even great strategies feel heavy. Energy disperses into side conversations, second-guessing, and quiet resignation. That's why belief isn't a "soft skill." It's a measurable source of velocity.

**Belief as a Cultural Currency**

In a company, belief is traded like currency.
Every conversation either deposits or withdraws from the collective bank of conviction.
When leadership delivers a vision with authenticity, it's a deposit. When they over-promise, under-deliver, or communicate without heart, it's a withdrawal.

Over time, those energetic transactions determine whether the company feels wealthy or bankrupt in spirit.
Healthy cultures have a high balance of belief. They can withstand uncertainty because they've built reserves of trust and emotional investment. Struggling cultures operate in deficit — every change feels like a threat because faith is fragile.

Belief, then, isn't just something employees have; it's something leaders cultivate.
It grows through integrity, transparency, and repetition.
The more consistent the energy behind a message, the stronger the collective field of belief becomes.

Belief is the bridge between vision and reality — and everyone in the company is a builder.

**Section 2: Leadership Belief — Conviction from the Top**

Every company is a mirror of its leadership's belief system.
The tone of a culture is set not by what executives say in meetings, but by what they believe in moments of uncertainty.

When leaders believe deeply in the mission — even when outcomes aren't guaranteed — that conviction becomes the organization's emotional anchor. It steadies people during change, emboldens creativity, and transforms challenges into invitations for growth.

Employees can sense belief the same way they sense authenticity. They may not be able to articulate it, but they can feel it. Energy doesn't lie.
A leader's belief — or doubt — radiates through tone, presence, and consistency.

When conviction is strong, it communicates safety:

"We know where we're going. We may not have every answer, but we trust the direction."

That frequency allows teams to move forward even amid ambiguity.

When conviction is weak, energy scatters.
Teams hold back ideas. Middle managers hesitate to make decisions. People spend more time interpreting leadership mood than advancing strategy. The company starts to wobble because its energetic core has lost balance.

## Belief as Emotional Leadership

True leadership belief isn't about charisma or confidence; it's about energetic coherence — the alignment between what a leader says, feels, and does.

Employees subconsciously track this alignment. When they sense consistency, they trust. When they sense contradiction, they doubt.

You can't fake belief. You can only embody it.

That embodiment requires leaders to move beyond motivation and into meaning — to reconnect personally with why they believe in the mission. Because when you believe for real, you don't have to sell it. You simply transmit it.

**The Belief Mirror Check**

A simple exercise for leaders:
Before any major presentation, decision, or announcement, pause and ask yourself three questions:

1. Do I genuinely believe in what I'm about to say?
2. Can I explain why it matters beyond metrics or obligation?
3. Does my energy — tone, posture, eye contact — reflect that belief?

If any answer feels hesitant, take a moment to realign before speaking. Your energy will communicate louder than your words ever could.

**Belief During Uncertainty**

Leadership belief is most visible in hard times.
It's easy to believe when results are good and growth is steady. It's during setbacks — product delays, market shifts, budget cuts — that teams look to leaders for energetic steadiness.

A leader who can say, "Yes, this is challenging, but I still believe in what we're building," transmits hope grounded in reality.
That balance of honesty and faith creates a vibration of trust that no motivational speech can replicate.

One CEO once told his staff during a difficult quarter:

"We may not hit every target, but we will not lose who we are in the process."

That single sentence carried more belief than an entire strategy deck. Because belief isn't about denying difficulty — it's about declaring direction in the face of it.

**The Ripple Effect**

When leaders hold belief, they become frequency setters for the entire organization.
Their calm becomes contagious. Their conviction becomes a permission slip for others to believe, too.
The result is a company that doesn't just chase goals but embodies them.

Leadership belief, therefore, is not optional — it's foundational.
It's the invisible signal that tells people whether to give their best energy or to protect it.

People don't follow plans. They follow conviction.
And conviction is belief, embodied.

**Section 3: Team Belief — Creating Collective Ownership**

Belief becomes powerful when it moves from one person's conviction to everyone's participation.
It's not enough for leaders to believe — teams must feel invited to believe with them.

A company becomes unstoppable when belief shifts from being a message to being a movement.
In that moment, employees stop working for the company and start working as the company. They see themselves as co-creators of the mission rather than executors of a plan.

## Belief as Belonging

At its essence, belief is a form of belonging.
People believe most deeply when they feel seen, valued, and trusted.
When they can see their fingerprints on the final outcome, ownership becomes emotional — not just professional.

That's why transparency and inclusion are essential ingredients for collective belief.
When teams understand not only the goals but why those goals exist, they stop questioning leadership intent and start fueling leadership direction.

You can't command belief — you have to cultivate it.
That happens through genuine connection, shared storytelling, and recognition of contribution.
Every "thank you," every "I couldn't have done this without you," adds another thread of belief to the cultural fabric.

## From Employees to Stakeholders of Energy

In traditional management, employees execute.
In conscious organizations, they energize.

Every team member is an energetic stakeholder — their enthusiasm, ideas, and care either strengthen or weaken the collective field of belief. When people see that their emotional energy matters, they start to self-regulate around alignment. They ask themselves, "Am I feeding the frequency or draining it?"

Ownership, then, is no longer just accountability — it's participation in the company's vibration.

## The Ownership Circle Exercise

A simple but transformative team practice:

1. Bring together 6–8 team members from different departments.

2. Ask each person to answer:

   o What part of our mission inspires me most?

   o How does my work contribute to that?

   o What part of our vision do I personally believe in most deeply?

3. Have each person share aloud.

What you'll notice is energy rising as people speak.
When belief is voiced collectively, it becomes amplified. Teams start to see how their unique contributions intersect — forming a unified circle of purpose.

At the end of the exercise, close by asking:

"What can we do, together, to protect this belief when things get hard?"

That question creates psychological safety and shared responsibility — a collective agreement that belief is not fragile, it's sacred.

**The Power of Shared Wins**

Belief grows through evidence.
Every small success — a satisfied client, a product improvement, a heartfelt testimonial — reinforces that the vision is working.

When leaders pause to celebrate those moments publicly, it's more than morale-boosting. It's belief-building.
Each acknowledgment becomes proof that the energy invested is creating results.

Belief compounds the same way interest does — when reinvested consistently, it multiplies exponentially.

## The Emotional Contract

At its core, belief between leadership and teams is a two-way agreement:

- Leaders promise to act with integrity and clarity.
- Teams promise to give their best energy in return.

This emotional contract can't be written, but it's felt. It creates a sense of "we" instead of "us and them." It dissolves departmental walls and invites cross-functional trust.

When everyone in the organization holds even a fraction of belief in the vision, that energy merges into something extraordinary — collective confidence.

## Energetic Takeaway

Belief becomes culture when it is shared.
It's not about perfect alignment or identical opinions; it's about emotional unity around a shared purpose.

The most successful teams don't just believe in their leaders — they believe in each other.

When belief is shared, energy multiplies. And when energy multiplies, culture becomes unstoppable.

## Section 4: Brand Belief — Turning Culture Outward

Every company radiates an energy field that reaches far beyond its office walls.
You can see it in the way a customer service email feels, in the tone of marketing copy, in how employees speak about their work after hours.

That energy is the company's brand — and it's powered entirely by internal belief.

A brand is not a logo, a slogan, or a color palette.
It's the emotional vibration that people experience when they encounter your organization.
It's the felt sense of who you are before a word is ever spoken.

And that feeling always originates inside.

When belief is strong internally, brand confidence ripples outward effortlessly.
Employees become natural ambassadors. Customers can sense authenticity. The company's communication feels consistent because it's coherent — not scripted.

When belief is weak, even the best marketing sounds hollow.
You can spend millions on messaging, but if employees don't believe it, the world won't either. Energy translates — and people can feel when a brand's words don't match its frequency.

**The Inside-Out Rule**

The energy of a brand mirrors the energy of its culture.
If the internal culture is confused, anxious, or misaligned, that dissonance leaks into every touchpoint — ads, sales calls, even product design.

But when belief thrives inside, brand storytelling becomes effortless.
You don't need to manufacture excitement; you simply amplify truth.

That's why great brands start with internal resonance before external reach. They invest in helping employees connect emotionally with the mission. They remind teams not just what they're selling, but why it matters.

Every employee who understands that "why" becomes part of the brand's living frequency — its human marketing engine.

## The Belief Continuum

There's a direct energetic continuum that connects leadership → culture → brand → customer.

1. **Leadership Belief** sets the tone.
2. **Team Belief** builds culture.
3. **Culture Belief** becomes brand energy.
4. **Customer Belief** becomes loyalty.

Break that continuum anywhere, and the energy flow stops.
But when belief is strong at every level, the company becomes magnetic — not just admired, but trusted.

## Story: The Brand That Rebuilt From Within

Several years ago, a mid-sized consumer company noticed its sales plateauing despite heavy marketing. The leadership team assumed they needed a new campaign. Instead, they conducted an internal listening tour and discovered that many employees no longer felt connected to the mission — "we used to believe in what we made, but now it's all about numbers."

Instead of rebranding externally, they started by rebuilding internally. Leadership shared honest town halls, rearticulated the company purpose, and invited employees to share what the brand meant to them.

Within six months, morale improved dramatically. Employees began posting their own stories on social media, celebrating the company's impact. Those authentic messages attracted more engagement than any paid campaign.

The result? Growth resumed — not because of a marketing refresh, but because belief had been restored.

**Exercise: The Inside-Out Audit**

To assess whether your external image matches your internal belief, try this:

- Gather a small group of employees.
- Ask them to describe the company in three words.
- Compare those words to your marketing tagline or brand promise.

If the internal and external language don't match, you've found your next alignment opportunity. The goal isn't to force uniformity, but to bridge the gap between the story you tell and the story your people live.

**Energetic Integrity**

A brand with energetic integrity feels like truth.
It doesn't overpromise; it delivers consistently from the inside out.
It's transparent, confident, and magnetic.

When your internal culture is filled with belief, you no longer need to convince customers. They can feel it.

Your brand is your belief made visible.
When culture believes, the world believes too.

## Section 5: Belief as a Performance Strategy

In most organizations, belief is treated as a "soft skill."
It's celebrated in posters, discussed at retreats, and forgotten in quarterly reviews. But in reality, belief is a hard driver of performance — one of the most powerful, yet least measured, forms of competitive advantage.

You can feel the performance difference between a team that believes and one that doesn't.
Believing teams move faster, collaborate better, and innovate with courage.
Disbelieving teams overanalyze, protect themselves, and play small.
The energy is entirely different — and so are the results.

Belief creates efficiency.
When people believe in the vision, they spend less time seeking validation and more time creating solutions. They stop asking, "Is this the right direction?" and start saying, "Let's make it happen."

That shift — from hesitation to ownership — is the moment belief becomes strategy.

### The Invisible KPI

Every company tracks revenue, retention, and market share.
But belief, though harder to quantify, underlies them all.

When belief is high:

- Engagement scores rise.

- Turnover falls.

- Productivity accelerates.

- Customer satisfaction improves.

- Innovation thrives.

When belief is low, the opposite unfolds — despite the best systems or incentives.
People disengage not because they're tired, but because they no longer see meaning in the effort.
They stop believing their energy will make a difference.

Belief acts like the current in an electrical system: invisible, but essential.
Without it, even the most advanced machinery won't run.

## The Neuroscience of Belief

From a biological perspective, belief literally changes performance potential.
When people believe in what they're doing, their brains release dopamine — the chemical associated with motivation, creativity, and resilience.
Dopamine helps teams stay focused through challenge and uncertainty.
It fuels the willingness to take risks, experiment, and persist.

Doubt, on the other hand, activates cortisol — the stress hormone that narrows focus and suppresses innovation.
That's why teams that believe can stay open and adaptive under pressure, while teams that doubt become rigid and reactive.

The science simply confirms what energy has always known: belief expands possibility.

## The Resilience Effect

Belief is also the foundation of resilience.
When setbacks happen — and they always do — belief determines whether people collapse or recalibrate.

A team grounded in belief sees obstacles as temporary. They interpret them as part of progress rather than proof of failure.
They ask, "What can we learn?" instead of "Why us?"
This mindset shortens recovery time and preserves emotional energy.

In contrast, disbelief magnifies challenges. Small issues become crises. Teams lose perspective because they no longer trust that their work leads anywhere meaningful.

In business terms, belief is the difference between momentum and stagnation.

## How Belief Drives Innovation

Innovation is, by definition, the act of believing something unseen into being.
It requires emotional safety — the ability to explore ideas without fear of failure or ridicule.

When leaders cultivate belief, they create psychological permission for creativity.
They signal: "We believe in your potential."
That belief becomes a field where ideas can emerge freely.

In environments of disbelief, people censor themselves.
They say what's safe instead of what's true.
The company stagnates not because it lacks talent, but because the energetic field of possibility has collapsed.

Belief expands that field.
It transforms fear into curiosity — the raw material of innovation.

## The Data Meets the Energy

Even the most data-driven organizations can trace performance back to emotional alignment.

A study by Gallup found that employees who "strongly believe" in their company's purpose are 4.5 times more likely to stay inspired at work. Another study by Deloitte revealed that purpose-driven companies outperform the market by 42% in long-term returns.

Behind those numbers lies energy — belief expressed as loyalty, enthusiasm, and creativity.

Belief may not appear on a balance sheet, but it shows up in every metric that matters.
It's not a variable; it's a multiplier.

Belief is the invisible KPI of every successful culture.
Measure it not in charts, but in the energy of your people.

## Section 6: Manifest This in Your Company — Exercises

Belief is built through repetition and evidence — not slogans.
It's the result of consistent alignment between words, actions, and energy.
The following practices help leaders and teams strengthen that alignment and turn belief into a daily operating rhythm.

### 1. Belief Mapping

**Purpose:** To uncover what your organization truly believes — not what it says it believes.

### How to do it:

- Bring your leadership team or department heads together.
- Draw three columns on a whiteboard labeled:
  **What We Say We Believe**, **What We Actually Do**, and **What We Want to Believe.**
- Ask participants to populate each column honestly.

The gaps between "say" and "do" are where belief needs recalibration. Discuss how to bridge those spaces through clearer communication, consistency, or new habits.

**Why it works:**
Belief mapping transforms abstract values into visible energy patterns. When misalignments are seen, they can be healed.

Belief isn't taught; it's remembered through alignment.

## 2. The Leadership Story Circle

**Purpose:** To reconnect leaders to their personal "why."

**How to do it:**

- Gather leaders or managers in a circle (no slides, no notes).
- Each person shares the moment they first believed in the company's mission — or what keeps them believing now.
- After each story, pause for a moment of silence before moving to the next.

By the end, the room feels alive with emotion and authenticity. Belief becomes tangible — spoken into the air and amplified by witness.

**Why it works:**
Stories are carriers of belief. They remind everyone that business is not about products or positions — it's about purpose shared through people.

## 3. The Belief Barometer

**Purpose:** To measure the collective conviction of your organization.

**How to do it:**
Once a quarter, send a simple, one-question survey:

"On a scale of 1 to 10, how strongly do you believe in our direction as a company?"

Follow up with one open-ended question:

"What would strengthen your belief even more?"

Review responses honestly.
This isn't a judgment — it's a mirror.
Belief rises when people feel heard and valued.

**Why it works:**
It transforms belief from an invisible feeling into a visible, trackable pulse of the organization.

## 4. Culture Amplifiers

**Purpose:** To integrate belief into daily habits and rituals.

**How to do it:**
Create small, consistent touchpoints that reinforce belief:

- Begin meetings with a 60-second story of success or customer impact.

- Celebrate milestones publicly, no matter how small.

- Acknowledge not just outcomes but acts of belief — someone who took a risk, spoke up, or tried something new.

Belief compounds when recognized. The act of noticing it multiplies it.

What you celebrate, you strengthen.

## 5. The Recommitment Ritual

**Purpose:** To renew collective belief after major transitions or challenges.

**How to do it:**

- Host an all-company session titled "What We Still Believe."
- Begin with a brief reflection from leadership on lessons learned.
- Then open the floor for team members to share one thing they still believe about the company's purpose.
- Capture the responses visually on a large board or digital canvas.

The final mosaic becomes a living portrait of resilience and unity. Even when the path changes, the core belief remains.

**Why it works:**
It reminds everyone that belief isn't fragile — it's the one thing that grows stronger when tested.

## Energetic Takeaway

Belief is both cause and effect.
The more you act from belief, the more evidence appears to sustain it.
It's not blind faith — it's energetic alignment with possibility.

Organizations don't need everyone to believe at 100%.
They just need enough people holding strong belief to shift the frequency of the whole system.

Belief multiplies through evidence. And evidence begins with action.

## Section 7: Reflection Prompts

Belief is both deeply personal and profoundly collective.
It's not something you can demand from others; it's something you
awaken within yourself and then model in your environment.

Use these reflection prompts as conversation starters, journaling
exercises, or end-of-meeting reflections. They're designed to re-center
everyone — from executives to new hires — around the question:
What do I believe, and how does that belief move through me into my
work?

### For Leaders

### 1. Where might I be overcommunicating vision but under-communicating belief?
Clarity explains what we're doing. Belief transmits why it matters. Do
my messages contain both, or do they lean too heavily on one?

### 2. Do my actions and energy align with what I say I believe?
When I speak about the mission, do I feel its truth in my body — or
am I repeating a practiced script? Where might I need to realign with
authenticity?

### 3. How do I respond to disbelief in others?
Do I meet skepticism with defense or curiosity? Every doubt in the
organization is an invitation to deepen clarity and trust.

### 4. What evidence can I provide that belief is working?
When was the last time I connected outcomes to energy — showing
the team that our faith in the mission creates tangible results?

### 5. Do I give myself permission to believe in something bigger than metrics?
Belief lives at the intersection of purpose and practicality. Am I making
space for both in my leadership decisions?

## For Teams

### 1. What part of our company's mission do I personally believe in most?

When do I feel proud to represent this organization, and what about that moment lights me up?

### 2. Where do I feel my belief wavering?

Is it due to miscommunication, burnout, or a lack of connection to the larger purpose? What would help reignite that spark?

### 3. How does my own energy influence the belief of those around me?

Am I contributing optimism, or unintentionally spreading doubt? Energy moves fast in a culture — awareness creates choice.

### 4. When have I seen belief create real results here?

Recall a time when the team's confidence carried a project to success. What can we learn from that experience?

### 5. What does belief feel like to me — emotionally and physically?

When I'm in belief, do I feel grounded, open, excited? How can I anchor that feeling more often throughout my day?

### Team Reflection Ritual

End a meeting or project debrief with this question:

"What do we believe today that we didn't believe six months ago?"

This practice encourages awareness of growth and progress. It helps teams see how belief evolves with evidence — turning faith into confidence and confidence into momentum.

## Energetic Reflection

Belief is a living frequency.
It ebbs and flows based on how often we nurture it with truth, gratitude, and evidence.
Your awareness of it — individually and collectively — is what keeps it alive.

Belief doesn't need to be perfect to be powerful. It only needs to be present.

## Section 8: Closing Affirmation

Belief is the current that carries a vision from imagination into reality.
It is invisible, but you can feel it in every conversation, every decision, every risk taken with heart.

It is the quiet confidence that says, "We can do this," long before proof arrives.
It's the collective inhale before a leap — the energy that bridges clarity and creation.

When belief flows through a company, culture becomes magnetic.
People show up differently — with light in their eyes and purpose in their work.
They collaborate without fear, innovate without needing permission, and recover from failure with grace.

Belief doesn't demand evidence — it creates it.
Every goal achieved, every product launched, every satisfied customer is a reflection of someone, somewhere, who chose to believe first.

So as you move forward, remember this:
You are not managing people. You are stewarding energy.
And the most powerful energy of all is belief.

Belief turns clarity into movement.
Movement turns culture into momentum.
Momentum turns companies into legacies.

# Chapter 3 — Emotional Alignment: The Pulse of Performance

## Section 1: The Energetics of Emotional Alignment

"Strategy organizes the mind; emotion energizes the mission."

Every organization runs on emotion — whether it admits it or not. Behind every spreadsheet, product launch, or quarterly goal lives a current of feeling: excitement, pressure, pride, anxiety, hope. Those emotions flow through meetings, emails, and hallways like an invisible network of electricity. When the current is strong and positive, the company hums. When it's blocked or negative, even the best strategies stall.

**Emotional alignment** is the harmony between how people feel and what the company is trying to create.
It is the point where individual energy synchronizes with collective purpose.
When that harmony exists, work feels effortless. Ideas flow, teams collaborate intuitively, and results seem to appear faster than they "should."

When it's missing, everything feels heavier.
Meetings drag. Small problems feel big. Communication becomes transactional. Employees check boxes instead of creating impact. The difference isn't intellect — it's vibration.

### The Hidden Performance Driver

One company can have identical resources, talent, and tools as another — yet produce radically different results. The differentiator isn't logic; it's emotion.
High-performing organizations pulse with trust, optimism, and curiosity. Struggling ones radiate tension, fear, and fatigue.

Emotion sets the energetic temperature.
When the climate is warm with connection and respect, people take risks, share ideas, and recover quickly from mistakes.
When the atmosphere turns cold with judgment or indifference, people withdraw, protect themselves, and creativity dies quietly in the corner.

**Energy in Motion**

Emotions are literally energy in motion.
They are the body's language for alignment — a real-time indicator of whether we're resonating with purpose or resisting it.
When a team feels inspired, its collective frequency rises.
Conversations move faster, ideas build instead of compete, and decisions are made from clarity rather than fear.

That's why emotional alignment is not "soft." It's structural.
It determines whether your organization is in flow or in friction.

Imagine two companies.
The first is financially successful but emotionally hollow. Employees perform well but feel unseen. Meetings are efficient but joyless.
Growth happens — but it drains rather than delights.
The second is smaller, maybe scrappier, but emotionally alive. People laugh in hallways. They challenge each other with respect. When setbacks happen, they regroup instead of retreat. Energy replenishes itself because emotional alignment creates renewable fuel.

Both achieve results — but only one is sustainable.

**Feeling as Feedback**

Every emotion inside an organization is feedback.
Excitement says "we're aligned."
Frustration says "something's off."
Apathy says "connection is missing."

When leaders listen without judgment, those feelings become data points — not problems to suppress, but messages to interpret.

Ignoring emotion doesn't neutralize it; it amplifies it underground. Addressing emotion with awareness clears energy and restores flow.

**The Pulse of Performance**

Emotional alignment is the pulse of performance — the rhythm that keeps a company's heart beating in time with its vision. When the pulse is strong, everything else — strategy, innovation, revenue — finds its natural tempo.

You don't have to manufacture motivation when people feel good. Positive emotion creates its own momentum.
It's the energetic equivalent of oxygen: invisible but essential.

Emotionally aligned companies don't chase culture; they embody it. They understand that behind every great brand, product, and customer experience is one simple truth: people who love what they're creating.

When leaders honor emotion as information and align feeling with purpose, work becomes less about managing and more about manifesting.

When energy flows through emotion, performance stops being forced and starts being fluent.

**Section 2: Leadership Energy — Emotional Awareness at the Top**

Every company is, at its core, an emotional ecosystem.
And like all ecosystems, its health depends on the quality of its environment — the air, the energy, and the tone that flows from the top down.

Leaders are the emotional thermostats of their organizations.
Their mood, body language, and energy quietly dictate the temperature
of the entire culture. When a leader is grounded, optimistic, and
transparent, people breathe easier. When they're reactive or closed off,
that energy ripples outward faster than any memo ever could.

Leadership, then, is not only about strategy — it's about energetic
stewardship.

## The Mirror Effect

Teams reflect the energy of their leaders.
If a leader is anxious, everyone feels it.
If a leader is hopeful, people mirror that tone in meetings and
decisions.
This phenomenon isn't mystical — it's neurological.

Humans are wired with mirror neurons that cause us to unconsciously
mimic the emotions and behaviors of those around us. When leaders
walk into a room, the team's emotional state adjusts almost instantly to
match their frequency.

That's why emotional awareness is the foundation of emotional
alignment.
You can't create resonance in others if you're dissonant within yourself.

Before leaders can regulate their teams, they must regulate their own
energy.

## Emotional Honesty as Leadership Strength

Old-school management taught that leaders should appear invulnerable
— calm, composed, unshaken. But in modern consciousness-driven
organizations, emotional honesty is the new executive strength.

Being emotionally aware doesn't mean being unfiltered; it means being real.

It's the ability to say, "Yes, this is challenging," without collapsing into negativity — to share truth while holding trust.

People don't expect perfection. They crave presence.

When leaders name emotions authentically — "I know many of us are feeling uncertain right now, and that's okay" — they release the collective tension that unspoken emotion creates.

It's not about fixing feelings; it's about acknowledging them so energy can move again.

**The Leadership Energy Scan**

A simple daily ritual to maintain emotional alignment:

1. **Pause before entering your workday.**
   Take a breath and ask, "What's the energy I'm bringing into the room today?"

2. **Identify it honestly.**
   Tired? Frustrated? Inspired? Neutral? There's no wrong answer. Awareness is the reset.

3. **Choose your broadcast.**
   Intentionally decide how you want to feel and what you want to project — calm confidence, focused enthusiasm, quiet optimism.

4. **Anchor it.**
   Before your first meeting, take one deep breath and imagine your chosen emotion expanding outward like light across the team.

This simple habit trains leaders to shift from reactive energy to intentional energy — from transmitting emotion unconsciously to doing so purposefully.

## Energy in Communication

Every leadership message carries two parts:
the content (the words) and the charge (the energy behind them).

Teams might forget the words, but they never forget the feeling. That's why the same strategy, delivered from frustration, can fall flat — while delivered from inspiration, it ignites.

Before presenting a vision or giving feedback, ask:

"Does my energy match the message I want to send?"

Alignment between tone and intention is what makes communication magnetic.

## The Ripple of Regulation

When leaders model emotional regulation, teams feel safe.
They learn that composure isn't detachment — it's stewardship.
Calm energy signals to others: We can handle this.

And that simple signal multiplies. Meetings run smoother. Conflict turns productive. Trust builds silently, one emotionally aware moment at a time.

Emotional awareness is not self-indulgence; it's organizational intelligence.

Because how a leader feels becomes how a company performs.

## Section 3: Team Alignment — Building Safety and Flow

If leadership sets the emotional tone, teams sustain the rhythm.
An organization's collective energy depends on whether its teams feel safe enough to express truth, contribute ideas, and show up authentically.

Emotional alignment thrives where there is psychological safety.
It's the invisible permission slip that says:

"You can be honest here. You can make mistakes here. You can care deeply here."

Without it, employees armor up. They say what sounds right instead of what feels real. Creativity shrinks. Meetings become performances instead of collaborations.

When people feel emotionally unsafe, they stop contributing their full selves — and that's when alignment fractures.
Because you can't align what people are afraid to reveal.

### The Trust Triangle

Healthy team energy follows a simple pattern — a cycle that continuously reinforces itself:

1. **Safety** → People feel accepted as they are.

2. **Expression** → They speak truthfully without fear of punishment.

3. **Engagement** → They invest emotionally in the outcome.

When that triangle is intact, energy circulates freely.
Ideas bounce without ego. Disagreements stay constructive because trust remains the foundation.

When any point weakens, the current breaks.
Silence replaces honesty. Teams spend more energy managing emotion than managing outcomes. The result is cultural stagnation — activity without alignment.

## The Feelings Round

A simple yet transformative practice to strengthen emotional safety:

At the start of important meetings, pause for 60 seconds and go around the room.
Each person shares one word describing how they're feeling in that moment.
No commentary. No fixing. Just listening.

The first time, it might feel awkward. But soon it becomes normal — even necessary.

What this does:

- It acknowledges emotion as valid data.

- It builds empathy across the team.

- It normalizes honesty, which opens creative flow.

When people are allowed to name emotion, they release it. The energy clears, and the meeting that follows is lighter, more focused, and far more connected.

## The Emotional Economy of Teams

In every team, emotions are exchanged like currency.
Encouragement, recognition, and appreciation are deposits.
Criticism without empathy, lack of acknowledgment, or passive avoidance are withdrawals.

Over time, those transactions determine whether the team feels wealthy or bankrupt in spirit.

The most successful teams invest consciously. They give feedback with care, celebrate each other's strengths, and recover quickly from tension. They understand that emotional energy is renewable when managed with awareness.

## Flow Through Connection

When a team reaches emotional alignment, it enters flow state — a collective momentum where time disappears and work feels effortless. This happens when trust, clarity, and passion intersect.

Everyone knows their role.
Communication is intuitive.
There's no need for micromanagement because people feel ownership, not obligation.

Leaders often describe these teams as "magical," but the magic is measurable — it's emotional coherence.

When emotion aligns with purpose, teams stop chasing motivation and start channeling energy.

## Example: The Team That Spoke Up

A mid-size tech company once struggled with low morale despite high performance. When surveyed anonymously, most employees said the same thing: "I don't feel safe speaking up."

The CEO replaced weekly status meetings with 30-minute "truth sessions" — open forums for sharing frustrations, ideas, and feelings. No repercussions, no defensiveness.

At first, conversations were tense. Then, slowly, humor and honesty returned.
Within six months, employee engagement scores rose by 38%.
The only thing that changed was permission.

When people were allowed to feel, they began to believe again.

Alignment begins when emotion is acknowledged, not avoided.
Safety is the soil from which performance grows.

## Section 4: The Business Impact — Emotional Energy as Performance Fuel

Most organizations try to manage performance through systems: metrics, KPIs, dashboards, and deadlines.
But what truly drives performance is not in the spreadsheet—it's in the space between people.

That space is emotional energy.
It's the trust in a handshake, the tone of an email, the warmth of collaboration, and the courage behind innovation.
When that energy flows cleanly, results accelerate.
When it's blocked by fear, fatigue, or disconnection, even the best systems struggle to move forward.

## Emotion as the Engine of Execution

We often treat emotion as something to manage, not to measure. But emotions are the engines of execution— fuel for decision-making, creativity, and endurance.
When teams are emotionally aligned, their cognitive performance expands. They think faster, empathize more deeply, and adapt to change with agility.

This isn't poetic—it's biological.
Positive emotions like curiosity, optimism, and gratitude trigger

dopamine and oxytocin—neurochemicals that enhance motivation, trust, and collaboration.
Negative emotions like fear and resentment trigger cortisol and adrenaline—chemicals meant for survival, not innovation.

One company might operate in a steady drip of adrenaline, always "pushing harder," while another functions through dopamine—focused, energized, and inspired.
The first burns out. The second builds momentum.

Performance isn't created by pressure—it's sustained by emotional alignment.

## The Return on Emotion (ROE)

Just as ROI measures the return on investment, ROE measures the return on emotion—the performance lift created when people feel connected, valued, and inspired.

Consider these correlations:

- Teams that report high emotional connection show up to 21% higher productivity.

- Employees who feel cared for are 17 times more likely to describe their company as "a great place to work."

- Companies with emotionally intelligent leadership outperform peers by 20–30% in profitability.

These aren't coincidences. They're the metrics of emotion in motion. When people feel seen and safe, their energy multiplies—because belief and emotion always compound each other.

## From Engagement to Energetic Coherence

Traditional engagement programs focus on external perks: benefits, outings, or recognition programs.
But emotional alignment goes deeper—it's internal coherence.

Coherence happens when heart and mind operate in sync.
In an aligned organization, communication between departments mirrors that same internal synchronization.

People know how their role connects to the whole.
They operate with empathy instead of ego.
The result? Faster problem-solving, clearer priorities, fewer misunderstandings.

It's not that emotion replaces strategy—it enhances it.
Strategy gives direction. Emotion gives propulsion.

Logic sets the course, but emotion is the wind that fills the sails.

## Resilience as a Competitive Edge

Emotional alignment also builds resilience—the quiet power to keep going when conditions shift.
A culture that prioritizes emotional wellbeing recovers faster from setbacks because people don't just depend on systems—they depend on each other.

In a world of constant change, emotional stability becomes the new form of consistency.
It keeps organizations creative instead of reactive, connected instead of defensive.

Resilient teams don't crumble when plans shift—they recalibrate.
Their emotional alignment gives them the flexibility to adapt without losing momentum.

## The Emotional Signature of Success

Every company has an emotional signature—a dominant feeling that defines its experience from the inside out.
It's the answer to the question: "What does it feel like to work here?"

For some, it's chaos.
For others, it's warmth, focus, and joy.

The most successful organizations are intentional about that emotional signature. They choose it, cultivate it, and protect it as fiercely as any trade secret.

Because emotion is not a byproduct of success—it's the source of it.

Emotional coherence turns ordinary teams into extraordinary ones.
It's the frequency where performance and purpose finally meet.

## Section 5: Manifest This in Your Company — Exercises

Emotional alignment doesn't happen by accident — it's cultivated through awareness, consistency, and practice.
These exercises are designed to help leaders and teams tune the emotional "frequency" of their workplace so that energy flows cleanly through every interaction, project, and decision.

### 1. Energy Mapping

**Purpose:** To identify the emotional hotspots and low points across your organization.

**How to do it:**

- Gather key team members or department heads.

- Draw an outline of your company's structure (or use a digital whiteboard).

- Ask participants to label each team, department, or process with one emotion that best describes its current energy. (Examples: motivated, anxious, inspired, overwhelmed, collaborative, disconnected.)

- Discuss what patterns emerge.

**The insight:**
High-energy areas reveal where alignment is strong; low-energy areas show where emotional disconnection may be draining performance. Don't label it as "good" or "bad" — treat it as energetic data.

You can't shift what you can't see — awareness creates flow.

**2. Emotion-to-Action Workshop**

**Purpose:** To help teams transform emotion into aligned behavior.

**How to do it:**

- Start a team meeting by asking: "What's the dominant emotion in our work right now?"

- Write responses on a board — positive or negative.

- For each emotion, brainstorm one action that would either amplify it (if positive) or transmute it (if negative).

**Example:**

- Emotion: "Overwhelmed."

- Action: "Let's pause non-essential meetings for one week."

- Emotion: "Excited."

- Action: "Share our progress with the rest of the company."

**The insight:**
Emotions are energy signals — this exercise trains people to respond consciously, turning emotional awareness into organizational intelligence.

Emotion is the raw material of transformation — if you listen to it.

## 3. The Gratitude Loop

**Purpose:** To raise the collective frequency through appreciation and acknowledgment.

**How to do it:**

- At the end of each day or week, invite everyone to send one short message of thanks to a colleague.
- Keep it specific ("I appreciate how you stayed late to help me finish the proposal") rather than general ("Thanks for everything").

Over time, this creates a ripple effect — a loop of recognition that restores energy faster than any corporate perk ever could.

**The insight:**
Gratitude shifts the brain's focus from scarcity to sufficiency. It rewires perception from "what's missing" to "what's working."

Gratitude is the shortest route to emotional realignment.

## 4. Resonance Reset Meetings

**Purpose:** To consciously maintain cultural and emotional alignment through reflection and recalibration.

**How to do it:**

- Once a month, dedicate a 45-minute meeting to energy, not strategy.
- Ask three simple questions:
    1. What's feeling good right now?
    2. What's feeling heavy or unclear?
    3. What's one shift we can make to restore flow?

Document the responses and revisit them next month.
This becomes your emotional balance sheet — a measure of how aligned the company feels.

**The insight:**
The most successful organizations treat emotional alignment as a rhythm, not a reaction.

Resonance doesn't require perfection — only awareness and recalibration.

## 5. The Emotion Board

**Purpose:** To make emotional awareness visible and part of the daily culture.

**How to do it:**

- Create a shared board or digital workspace labeled: "How's our energy today?"
- Encourage people to post short reflections, emojis, or images representing their current emotion.
- Review the board weekly to see shifts in tone.

**The insight:**
When emotion becomes part of the conversation, it stops controlling the culture from the shadows.

Emotional transparency builds collective strength.

## Energetic Takeaway

Alignment is not the absence of emotion — it's the intelligent flow of it.
When teams are invited to feel, name, and channel emotion constructively, they no longer leak energy through stress or conflict. Instead, they create a self-sustaining cycle of emotional awareness, trust, and creativity.

Emotion fuels motion.
Alignment turns motion into momentum.

## Section 6: Reflection Prompts

Emotional alignment begins with self-awareness.
Before a company can manage its culture, each individual must understand their own energetic patterns — how they feel, how they respond, and how their emotional state influences others.

Use these questions to check in with yourself and your team.
They can be used as journaling prompts, one-on-one coaching reflections, or closing questions in weekly meetings.

### For Leaders

### 1. How emotionally aware am I of my team?
Do I notice the emotional tone of meetings, or am I too focused on tasks? When was the last time I paused to ask, "How are you really doing?"

**2. What emotion do I bring into the room most often?**
Calm? Urgency? Doubt? Enthusiasm?
Every leader broadcasts an emotional frequency — what's mine, and is it helping or hindering alignment?

**3. Do I model emotional honesty or emotional control?**
Am I trying to appear "strong," or am I demonstrating real strength through transparency, empathy, and grounded calm?

**4. When do I feel most aligned in my work?**
Identify moments when leadership feels natural and energized. What emotions are present then, and how can I recreate them more intentionally?

**5. How do I restore my energy when I feel emotionally drained?**
Awareness is only powerful when paired with renewal. What rituals — breathing, walking, silence, gratitude — bring me back into coherence?

**For Teams**

**1. How safe do I feel expressing emotion at work?**
Can I disagree respectfully? Can I share when something feels off? If not, what would help me feel more comfortable being honest?

**2. How does the team respond to emotion?**
When someone shows frustration or excitement, do we lean in with curiosity or pull away with discomfort?

**3. What emotions dominate our daily interactions?**
Are we operating mostly in stress, urgency, and caution — or in creativity, trust, and optimism?

**4. When did our team feel most connected recently?**
What was happening in that moment — laughter, collaboration, shared success? What can we learn from that state of flow?

### 5. How can I contribute to emotional balance?

What's one way I can help calm, inspire, or ground the team when energy feels off? Small emotional adjustments often create the biggest cultural impact.

### Teams Pulse Moment

At the end of each week, take two minutes to answer collectively:

"How did our culture feel this week?"

Record one word or phrase.
Over time, this becomes a living emotional timeline — a mirror of your company's evolving frequency.

When the team feels balanced and optimistic, you'll notice creativity rising. When the tone feels heavy or flat, it's time for recalibration.

Emotions are always giving feedback — all you have to do is listen.

### Energetic Reflection

Emotional alignment isn't about controlling feelings; it's about honoring them as guidance systems.
When you allow emotion to be felt, named, and redirected with intention, you move from reaction to resonance.

Your emotional awareness is your energetic intelligence.
The more you feel consciously, the more powerfully you lead.

### Section 7: Closing Affirmation

Emotion is the pulse of every organization —
a rhythm that beats beneath every decision, meeting, and dream.

It is the invisible signal that tells people whether to lean in or pull back, to speak up or stay silent, to give their best energy or simply get through the day.

When emotion flows freely, work becomes something more than work —

it becomes art, connection, and creation.
Ideas move faster. Collaboration deepens.
The company begins to hum in harmony with its own heartbeat.

Emotional alignment is not about chasing positivity;
it's about embracing truth.
It's the courage to feel what's real,
the wisdom to name it,
and the leadership to channel it into purpose.

When leaders listen with empathy,
when teams communicate with openness,
and when people feel seen for who they truly are —
the organization's energy rises to a higher frequency.
It becomes magnetic.

Because emotion is energy in motion —
and when that energy is aligned with clarity and belief,
it becomes unstoppable.

**When we feel good, we perform brilliantly.**
**When we align how we feel with what we create,**
**performance stops being forced and starts being fluent.** Emotion is not the opposite of business.
It is the essence of it.

# Chapter 4 — Inspired Action: From Compliance to Creativity

### Section 1: The Energetics of Inspired Action

"Action without inspiration is movement without meaning. Inspiration turns work into creation."

Action alone doesn't create transformation — aligned action does. Every company is full of activity: meetings, tasks, deliverables, endless checklists. But not all motion is progress. Some movement drains energy; some movement expands it. The difference lies in inspiration.

**Inspired action** is movement that originates from alignment — where belief, clarity, and emotion merge into momentum. It's when people act not because they have to, but because they want to. When employees feel connected to purpose, their actions are infused with creativity, ownership, and energy. Work stops being mechanical and becomes meaningful.

Forced action feels heavy. Inspired action feels alive.
The body knows the difference. The energy in the room knows the difference. So do customers.

### Action vs. Alignment

In many organizations, action is used as proof of productivity.
We equate motion with success — the fuller the calendar, the better the results. But constant movement without alignment leads to burnout, frustration, and diminishing returns.

Alignment, however, amplifies action.
When the emotional and energetic field of a company is coherent — when people understand why they're doing what they're doing — one inspired action can produce more impact than a hundred forced ones.

It's not about doing more; it's about doing what resonates.

Inspired action doesn't push — it pulls.
It draws people forward naturally because the energy behind it feels expansive, not pressured.

## The Frequency of Flow

When a team is aligned emotionally and energetically, action becomes effortless.
Meetings flow. Communication sharpens. Ideas seem to "appear" at the perfect moment. That's not luck — it's resonance.

Flow state in business is simply collective inspiration — the moment when effort meets enthusiasm.
In that state, employees don't need constant supervision; they're self-propelled by purpose. The workday feels lighter because people are acting in harmony with what they believe in.

Leaders who understand energy know this:
You can't motivate someone indefinitely through fear or deadlines.
You can only sustain momentum through inspiration.

## The Physics of Inspired Action

Inspired action follows the same laws as energy itself: it seeks the path of least resistance.
When clarity and belief are in place, energy naturally moves into form — ideas turn into projects, visions become results. There's no struggle or strain; the process feels guided.

But when clarity or belief is missing, action becomes forced — like trying to swim upstream. Progress still happens, but it costs more energy than it should.
That's why emotionally aligned organizations move faster: they're operating in energetic flow rather than friction.

Inspired action is the bridge between inner alignment and outer achievement.

## Compliance vs. Creativity

Compliance is the lowest vibration of action.
It's when people do the bare minimum — checking boxes, avoiding mistakes, staying safe.
Creativity is the highest vibration — when people feel empowered to take initiative, contribute ideas, and improve the system rather than simply follow it.

The energetic leap from compliance to creativity happens the moment people reconnect to meaning.
When employees see how their role contributes to the greater mission, their energy rises. They begin to act not just as workers, but as co-creators of success.

That shift changes everything.
Products improve. Customer experiences deepen. Innovation accelerates.
Because when inspiration fuels action, excellence becomes instinctive.

## Living Example: The Shift from Obligation to Ownership

A marketing agency once struggled with morale. Deadlines were met, but enthusiasm was gone.
After conducting internal interviews, leadership realized that employees no longer felt connected to why their work mattered. They were executing campaigns — not creating impact.

Instead of pushing harder, the company paused.
They redefined their mission: "We don't make ads — we tell stories that move people."
Suddenly, teams began generating ideas faster, laughing more, taking

bolder creative risks. Energy returned.
Same team. Same resources. Different vibration.

That's the power of inspired action.
It's not about doing more; it's about reconnecting the heart to the hands.

When clarity shows the way and belief fuels the spirit, inspired action becomes inevitable.
It's the energetic language of manifestation in motion — where thought becomes thing, and purpose becomes performance.

Inspired action is not work. It's energy expressing itself through you.

## Section 2: Leadership as the Catalyst for Inspiration

Inspiration is contagious — but only when it's authentic.
Employees can feel when leaders are aligned with purpose, just as they can sense when those leaders are disconnected, drained, or simply "managing."

Leaders don't inspire through words alone — they inspire through frequency.
Their tone, pace, presence, and energy speak louder than any mission statement on the wall.
Because leadership is not just about giving direction — it's about being a transmission.

When leaders are connected to their own inspiration, they don't need to demand productivity; their energy naturally lifts the room.
People start matching that vibration — not because they're told to, but because they want to.

Inspiration can't be demanded — it must be demonstrated.

## From Driving to Inviting

Many leaders unknowingly operate in "drive mode."
They push outcomes, apply pressure, and set unrelenting targets. On the surface, this approach seems effective — deadlines are met, goals are achieved.
But over time, it erodes the very energy that sustains creativity.

Driving energy communicates mistrust: "You wouldn't act unless I pushed."
Inviting energy communicates confidence: "I trust that you'll act when you're ready."

The difference between the two is subtle but profound.
One exhausts; the other empowers.
One creates compliance; the other unlocks creativity.

In inspired cultures, leaders don't chase action — they create the conditions where action flows.

**The Energetic Modeling Effect**

People don't follow what you say; they follow what you radiate.
This is why the most inspiring leaders are often the calmest. Their grounded energy creates stability, and their passion sparks curiosity.

A leader who is aligned with their mission doesn't have to sell it — they embody it.
They move with clarity, they speak with purpose, and their actions feel congruent.
That congruence is what earns trust — and trust is the soil in which inspiration grows.

When leaders act from alignment, everyone around them remembers what alignment feels like.

## Story: The 10-Minute Shift

A CEO of a design firm once noticed her team dragging through morning meetings. The updates were routine, the tone transactional. One day, she walked in and said, "We're going to start differently. Tell me one thing that inspired you this week — in work or life."

The energy in the room transformed instantly.
Someone shared about a podcast that sparked a new idea. Another spoke about a client's reaction to their project. Within minutes, laughter and energy filled the space.

That 10-minute ritual became permanent.
Productivity rose, but more importantly — people started showing up as their full selves again.

Inspiration didn't come from an initiative or incentive; it came from leadership energy that made space for it.

## The Power of Permission

Leaders often underestimate the power of granting permission. Permission to slow down, to think differently, to question, to feel inspired again.

When a leader says, "You have full permission to create," they remove the invisible tension that limits innovation.
People move from performing to expressing.

That permission shifts a culture from one of fear to one of flow. Because nothing blocks inspiration faster than the belief that it's not allowed.

## Energetic Leadership Practices

To activate inspiration through leadership:

1. **Pause before you push.** Ask, "Am I driving or inviting?"

2. **Share your own spark.** Talk about what excites you, not just what's urgent.

3. **Acknowledge emotional energy.** If the team feels off, name it and reset before forcing momentum.

4. **Protect inspired space.** Block time for brainstorming without agendas. Inspiration needs room to breathe.

## The Leadership Frequency

When leaders operate from inspiration rather than obligation, they change the electromagnetic field of the organization.
They set a tone of ease and enthusiasm that ripples through every conversation, client interaction, and decision.

That's how leadership becomes energetic — not managerial.

A leader in alignment becomes a lighthouse.
They don't chase ships; they shine so others can find their way.

## Section 3: Cultivating a Culture of Initiative

When inspiration is alive, initiative follows naturally.
In fact, initiative is simply inspired action at scale — it's what happens when individuals trust their own creativity enough to act without waiting for permission.

In a culture of initiative, people don't just complete tasks — they co-create progress. They bring ideas forward, challenge the status quo, and feel personally responsible for outcomes.
That level of ownership isn't taught; it's activated.

But to activate it, companies must release the illusion of control and embrace the intelligence of trust.

## Control vs. Creativity

Traditional management thrives on control. It believes that oversight creates order.
But too much control suffocates inspiration. It turns creators into executors and transforms engagement into compliance.

Creative organizations, on the other hand, operate on trust.
They believe that when people feel empowered, they regulate themselves through pride and purpose — not pressure.

Control says, "Don't make mistakes."
Creativity says, "Let's learn from what happens."

The difference between the two is the difference between fear and freedom — and only one of those states can produce inspired action.

Micromanagement kills momentum. Trust multiplies it.

## The 80/20 Empowerment Rule

To build a culture of initiative, leaders must intentionally share ownership.

Try this framework:

- **Leaders provide 20% direction** — the clarity, purpose, and desired outcome.
- **Teams own 80% of the approach** — the how, the pace, the creative method.

This balance ensures alignment without suffocating autonomy. It communicates, "We trust your intelligence."

And when people feel trusted, they rise to meet that belief.
They begin thinking like owners, not employees.

**The Permission Shift**

Most employees are conditioned to seek approval — to make sure their ideas are "safe" before acting.
But waiting for permission kills innovation faster than failure ever could.

Inspired companies flip the script. They tell employees:

"You already have permission — until you have a reason to ask for it."

This single statement unlocks massive creative energy.
People move faster, experiment more, and feel intrinsically motivated.

Because permission isn't just policy — it's energy. It signals freedom, trust, and possibility.

**Story: The Empowered Team**

A homebuilding company once discovered that their customer satisfaction scores were dropping, despite strong sales. Instead of launching a new system, leadership asked front-line employees what they thought was wrong.

Their response was clear: "We know what the customers want, but our processes are too rigid for us to make it happen."

The company removed several layers of approval and empowered sales agents to make certain decisions on the spot. Within three months, satisfaction scores soared.
The system didn't need to be smarter — the people did.

When they were trusted, they became unstoppable.

When people feel trusted, they move from doing their job to creating their work.

## The Role of Psychological Ownership

Initiative thrives when people feel that their contribution matters — that their fingerprints are on the outcome.
This is called psychological ownership.
It's the moment when "the company" becomes "my company."

Leaders can cultivate this feeling by:

- Sharing credit publicly.

- Giving teams autonomy over decision-making.

- Connecting each role back to the larger mission.

- Inviting input early in the creative process, not after decisions are made.

Ownership is emotional, not contractual.
When people care personally, performance takes care of itself.

## Energy Flows Where Permission Grows

In every organization, there's a moment when an employee thinks, "Should I do this, or should I wait?"
That's the point where inspiration either dies or ignites.

Cultures of initiative make it clear: act when it feels right, create when it feels inspired.
They'd rather course-correct creativity than manage complacency.

The future belongs to companies that lead through trust — because trust is the ultimate productivity tool.

## Section 4: The Business Impact — When Energy Becomes Execution

Every business wants faster execution, higher innovation, and better results.
But most companies chase those outcomes backward — they push harder, add more systems, tighten deadlines, and mistake busyness for momentum.

The truth is simple:
When energy is aligned, execution becomes effortless.
When it's misaligned, no amount of pressure can create flow.

### From Effort to Efficiency

Inspired action is the most efficient form of work because it eliminates resistance.
People don't waste energy doubting, defending, or delaying — they simply do.
They're not waiting for external validation; they're acting from internal conviction.

This energetic coherence shows up in practical ways:

- Projects move faster because teams communicate intuitively.
- Less time is spent in meetings clarifying direction.
- Innovation happens spontaneously instead of by mandate.
- Clients feel the enthusiasm and respond with loyalty.

Execution becomes an extension of inspiration.

Alignment is the new efficiency.

When people are in alignment with purpose, every action carries more power — like a perfectly tuned instrument producing pure sound.

## Alignment Velocity

Traditional business metrics measure speed in output.
Energetic businesses measure speed in alignment velocity — how quickly ideas move from concept to completion when energy flows without friction.

When belief, emotion, and clarity are aligned, momentum builds on its own. Teams enter a state of collective flow, where progress compounds naturally.

You'll notice it not in spreadsheets, but in sensations:
Meetings that end with enthusiasm instead of exhaustion.
Deadlines that are met early because people are excited to deliver.
Solutions that arise seemingly out of nowhere.

It's not magic — it's resonance.

When energy aligns, execution accelerates.

## Creativity as Currency

In a world of automation and AI, creativity is the last true competitive advantage.
Inspired action is what keeps that creativity alive.
You can't outsource innovation — it comes from people who feel emotionally invested in what they're creating.

Companies that cultivate inspiration become magnets for talent and ideas.
Their cultures buzz with curiosity, and their products carry a frequency that customers can feel.

When employees act from inspiration, their work radiates authenticity — and authenticity sells.

Creativity isn't just culture-building; it's revenue-generating.

**The Financial Ripple of Inspiration**

Inspired action affects every measurable business outcome:

- **Speed:** Teams in flow complete projects up to 50% faster.
- **Quality:** Intrinsic motivation produces higher craftsmanship.
- **Retention:** Inspired employees are five times more likely to stay.
- **Profit:** Purpose-driven companies outperform peers by over 40% in long-term returns.

These numbers tell a story that emotion and energy have always known:
Belief drives engagement.
Engagement drives action.
Action drives results.

The most successful companies don't chase productivity — they cultivate inspiration.

The fastest results come from the most aligned energy.

**When Work Becomes Art**

When inspired action becomes a way of operating, work transcends performance — it becomes artistry.
Employees aren't simply fulfilling roles; they're expressing something within themselves through their craft.

That's what customers respond to.
They don't just buy the product — they feel the energy behind it.

A company acting from inspiration emits a kind of invisible light.
It attracts opportunity, partnership, and loyalty because it feels alive.

That's the true business case for inspiration:
It doesn't just move numbers — it moves people.

## Energetic Truth

Execution is the physical expression of belief.
When inspiration fuels action, action fuels expansion.
That's how organizations grow — not just in revenue, but in resonance.

Inspired companies don't hustle; they harmonize.
They don't chase success; they attract it.

## Section 5: Manifest This in Your Company — Exercises

Inspired action thrives in environments that encourage freedom, meaning, and momentum.
These practices are designed to awaken creativity, reduce friction, and restore energetic flow — so that every initiative, project, and conversation begins from alignment rather than obligation.

## 1. The Inspiration Audit

**Purpose:** To reveal where in your organization energy is being fueled versus forced.

## How to do it:

- Gather department heads or team leaders.

- On a whiteboard, create two columns: Inspired and Required.
- Ask:
  "Which of our current projects feel naturally exciting, and which feel like we're pushing uphill?"
- Discuss what makes the inspired projects feel different. What energy, freedom, or purpose do they have that the others lack?

**Insight:**
Forced action drains energy because it's rooted in fear or expectation. Inspired action replenishes energy because it's rooted in meaning.

Inspiration is efficiency disguised as enthusiasm.

## 2. The Alignment Brief

**Purpose:** To anchor every project in purpose before it begins.

**How to do it:**
Before launching any new initiative, hold a 10-minute meeting where the only question discussed is:

"Why does this matter?"

Have each person share their perspective.
When the collective "why" is voiced, the group's emotional and energetic frequency rises — creating shared alignment before a single task begins.

**Insight:**
Most misalignment happens because teams forget the "why."
This exercise reconnects action to purpose — turning projects into missions.

Purpose is the fuel. Action is the flame.

## 3. Autonomy Zones

**Purpose:** To reawaken ownership and innovation through freedom.

**How to do it:**

- Choose one area of work — product design, customer experience, marketing strategy, etc.
- Give a small team full creative authority for 30 days.
- No approvals, no micromanagement — just freedom with accountability.

At the end, have the team share what they learned, what worked, and what they'd change.
The outcome is often secondary to the energy shift: confidence, collaboration, and creative flow all rise dramatically.

**Insight:**
Autonomy breeds responsibility — not chaos.
When people feel trusted, they naturally self-correct and self-inspire.

Freedom is the oxygen of inspiration.

## 4. Momentum Mapping

**Purpose:** To identify where action feels forced and where it flows.

**How to do it:**

- Once a month, ask your team to reflect on their projects using two categories:
    - **Flow:** Tasks or initiatives that feel exciting, clear, energizing.

- o **Friction:** Tasks that feel draining, confusing, or repetitive.

- Discuss what makes the flow projects work — is it clarity, teamwork, autonomy, or belief in the outcome?

Then explore how to apply those same energetic qualities to the friction areas.

**Insight:**
You don't always need a new process — just a new energy pattern.

Momentum is a mirror of energy: when it slows, something is misaligned.

## 5. The Inspiration Stand-Up

**Purpose:** To infuse the workday with energy before it begins.

**How to do it:**

- Begin your weekly team meeting with one question: "What's inspiring you this week — inside or outside of work?"

- Allow open sharing — it can be a book, a customer story, a family moment, or a personal win.

The goal isn't to analyze; it's to lift the collective frequency.
When energy rises, action follows effortlessly.

**Insight:**
People don't need new tasks; they need new energy.
When you start meetings with inspiration instead of status, everything changes.

Energy first. Execution second.

## Energetic Takeaway

Inspiration doesn't happen by accident — it happens by design.
When organizations prioritize energy alignment as much as strategic
alignment, they discover a new rhythm of success: one that's fast,
fulfilling, and sustainable.

The greatest leaders don't force action — they activate it.

When belief becomes emotion and emotion becomes action,
you're no longer managing performance — you're manifesting it.

## Section 6: Reflection Prompts

Inspired action begins with inner alignment.
Before creativity can move through a company, it must move through
people — through their beliefs, emotions, and intentions.
Use these reflection prompts to reconnect with your energy, clarify
motivation, and reignite purpose before you act.

### For Leaders

**1. Do I motivate through pressure or through inspiration?**
When I lead, do I ignite energy — or drain it through urgency?
Pressure might move people once; inspiration moves them indefinitely.

**2. Am I acting from alignment or expectation?**
Before making a decision or setting a goal, do I pause to ask, "Does
this feel aligned with our purpose, or am I forcing it from fear or
habit?"

**3. How often do I share my own inspiration with my team?**
Do they know what drives me, what lights me up, what I believe in?
Leadership energy becomes magnetic when it's personal and
transparent.

**4. What's one process or rule I could release to create more flow?**
Sometimes the most inspiring leadership act is to remove something —
a bottleneck, an unnecessary approval step, or a fear-based policy.

**5. Do I celebrate initiative as much as I correct mistakes?**
Every time I praise courageous action, I strengthen the field of
creativity within the culture.

Leaders don't create inspiration — they uncover it by removing fear.

**For Teams**

**1. When do I feel most alive at work?**
What kind of projects, people, or moments bring me energy rather
than drain it? What do those moments have in common?

**2. What would I do differently if I trusted my instincts more?**
If fear of judgment disappeared, what idea or improvement would I
bring forward tomorrow?

**3. How do I respond to direction — with excitement or
resistance?**
If resistance shows up, is it because I disagree, or because I don't feel
emotionally connected to the purpose behind the action?

**4. When was the last time I acted from inspiration rather than
obligation?**
How did that feel in my body? How did others respond to my energy?

**5. What's one inspired action I can take this week — no matter
how small?**
Maybe it's sharing a new idea, expressing gratitude, or improving a
customer experience.
Inspiration expands through consistency, not intensity.

You don't have to wait for inspiration to strike. You can choose to live inspired.

## Team Momentum Check

At the end of each week, gather your team and reflect together:

"What inspired action did we take this week — and what evidence of alignment showed up because of it?"

Keep a running list. Over time, you'll see a pattern emerge — proof that when energy moves with intention, results multiply effortlessly.

## Energetic Reflection

Inspiration is the bridge between vision and manifestation.
When leaders and teams honor their emotions, trust their instincts, and move with meaning, they enter a creative current where action becomes effortless.

You don't need to chase motivation — you need to clear space for it.

When your energy is aligned with your intention, inspired action becomes your default state.

## Section 7: Closing Affirmation

Action is the language of belief.
It is how energy becomes visible, how ideas take shape, how dreams become deliverables.
But not all action is equal.

Some action is mechanical — born from obligation, routine, or fear.
It gets things done, but it drains the spirit in the process.

And then there is inspired action — movement that feels effortless because it's born from alignment.
It doesn't push. It pulls.
It doesn't exhaust. It expands.

Inspired action is what happens when clarity fuels direction, belief fuels courage, and emotion fuels creativity.
It is the natural outflow of an organization that is alive — pulsing with trust, purpose, and possibility.

When a company reaches that state, everything accelerates.
Decisions become intuitive.
Innovation feels inevitable.
And success stops being chased — it starts arriving.

**Inspired action is energy in motion,
belief in practice,
and purpose made visible.**

It is the difference between activity and artistry,
between pressure and power,
between doing business and creating impact.

So as you lead, create, and collaborate, remember this:
Your energy precedes your action.
Your alignment determines your outcome.

And when your actions are inspired —
the universe conspires.

# Chapter 5 — Detachment: The Paradox of Power

## Section 1: The Energetics of Detachment

"True power isn't in holding tighter — it's in trusting that what you've built will rise on its own."

Most people misunderstand detachment.
They think it means caring less, pulling away, or becoming indifferent.
But detachment is not the absence of care — it's the presence of trust.

It's the energetic confidence that says, "I've done my part. Now I allow the process to unfold."

In business, that shift is profound.
When companies cling too tightly to outcomes — revenue targets, market share, public perception — their energy constricts. Innovation dries up. Employees start operating from fear instead of flow.
But when leadership relaxes into trust, the organization begins to breathe again.

**Detachment isn't disconnection. It's energetic alignment without resistance.**
It's the point where control gives way to confidence.

## The Law of Flow

Energy can't move freely through systems that are rigid.
In physics, this is called resistance — the force that slows current.
In business, it looks like overplanning, overthinking, and overmanaging.

When leaders try to control every outcome, they unknowingly block the very flow they're trying to create.
But when they trust their vision, their people, and the process, energy begins to move organically — faster, lighter, and more intelligently than logic could design.

Detachment, therefore, is not passive. It's the highest form of active faith.

Detachment is the space that allows possibility to breathe.

It's the pause between effort and outcome — the stillness that lets results crystallize.

## The Paradox of Power

Here lies the paradox:
The more tightly we grip, the more power slips through our fingers.
The moment we release control, everything begins to align.

Think of detachment as energetic equilibrium — the point where the company's desire for success is perfectly balanced by its willingness to trust the process.
That balance creates magnetic power.

When you act with confidence but remain unattached to how or when results appear, you unlock infinite possibility. You invite synchronicity, innovation, and unexpected solutions — because your energy is open to receiving, not constricted by fear.

**Story: The Over-Managed Launch**

A creative agency once spent months micromanaging every detail of a client's campaign. Every headline was debated, every email revised, every post approved by three layers of leadership. By the time it launched, the energy behind the project was stale.

When results underperformed, the CEO made a radical change: she gave the next campaign full creative freedom. The team felt trusted. They moved fast, took risks, and infused the work with excitement.

The outcome? The second campaign tripled engagement — with half the meetings.

The only difference was energetic detachment.
The company stopped controlling creativity and started trusting it.

**Energetic Neutrality**

Detachment is emotional maturity in motion.
It's being fully invested but not energetically dependent.
It's doing your best without needing the universe to prove you're right.

When organizations operate from this frequency, they become unstoppable — not because they force outcomes, but because they no longer block them.

They act with precision, then release with peace.
They work hard, but they don't carry the weight of worry.
They trust that what is aligned will unfold at the right time, in the right way.

Detachment doesn't weaken your intention — it strengthens your magnetism.

Because what you release with faith always returns with clarity.

**The Energetic Equation of Detachment**

Effort + Trust = Flow
Control + Fear = Friction

That's the essence of this principle.
Detachment is the energetic bridge between creation and manifestation — the point where you stop pushing and start allowing.

When individuals, leaders, and teams reach this state, the company itself begins to vibrate differently.
There's a sense of ease, confidence, and quiet power.
Deadlines feel lighter. Creativity feels freer. Relationships feel stronger.

Because detachment doesn't mean you stop caring — it means you start trusting that what you care about is already working.

True detachment isn't letting go of the goal.
It's letting go of the tension around it.

**Section 2: Leadership and the Illusion of Control**

In leadership, control often masquerades as strength.
It's the comfort of knowing every detail, approving every decision, being copied on every email.
But underneath that control is usually fear — fear of failure, fear of chaos, fear of not being needed.

And fear is always the opposite of flow.

Great leadership is not about control — it's about conscious direction.
It's about holding a clear intention and allowing talented people the
space to express it in their own way.

The more control you need, the less power you actually have.

**The Leadership Paradox**

At first, control feels productive.
It creates predictability. It produces quick results.
But over time, it suppresses the very energy that sustains growth —
creativity, autonomy, and trust.

Employees stop thinking for themselves.
They wait for approval instead of acting from initiative.
Innovation slows because people are afraid of doing it "wrong."

The leader becomes the bottleneck, not the bridge.

True leaders understand this paradox and step back just enough for
others to step forward.
They guide energy — they don't grip it.

**Micromanagement vs. Energetic Leadership**

Micromanagement is the physical expression of energetic attachment.
It's the belief that outcomes require control rather than alignment.

Energetic leadership, on the other hand, operates from trust.
It knows that once clarity, belief, and emotion are established, action will take care of itself.
It doesn't need to monitor every step — it simply maintains the vibration of confidence.

Energetic leaders understand that their role is not to manage effort, but to manage energy.
When their own energy is steady, they become the calm center that stabilizes everyone else.

Micromanagement says, "I don't trust you."
Energetic leadership says, "I trust the process."

## Story: The Leader Who Let Go

A senior executive at a national homebuilding company was known for her meticulous oversight. Every report crossed her desk. Every design required her approval. Her teams respected her — but they were exhausted.

One quarter, she faced an overwhelming number of simultaneous projects and had no choice but to delegate fully. She set the vision, then stepped back completely.

What happened surprised her.
Her teams didn't collapse — they soared.
They began collaborating faster, solving problems before they reached her inbox, and producing some of the most innovative work in the company's history.

For the first time, she saw the truth: her control had been slowing them down.
Her detachment became their empowerment.

## From Managing to Manifesting

When leaders release control, something profound happens — the organization begins to self-organize.
Ideas find their way to the right people.
Challenges surface naturally and are solved by those closest to the problem.
Energy begins to flow where it's most needed.

This isn't chaos; it's intelligence.
The system becomes responsive rather than rigid.

Leaders who operate in detachment focus less on "What's everyone doing?" and more on "What's the energy we're creating together?"

Because culture isn't managed — it's manifested through example.

## The Energetic Posture of Power

Power doesn't come from control; it comes from composure.
When leaders hold steady energy, their teams feel safe to innovate.
When they remain calm in uncertainty, others find clarity.

True leadership is energetic sovereignty — the ability to hold faith in the vision without needing to force the timeline.

When you stop needing to control everything,
you become the one thing everyone trusts.

That's the paradox of power:
The less you grasp, the more naturally things fall into place.

## Section 3: Emotional Intelligence in Detachment

Detachment without emotional intelligence can look like apathy.
But when guided by awareness, it becomes the most advanced form of
emotional mastery a leader can embody.

Emotional intelligence is the ability to feel deeply without being ruled
by feeling.
It's the inner balance point between empathy and equanimity — caring
fully while staying centered.

Detachment is what happens when emotional intelligence matures.
It's not disengagement; it's discernment.
It's the quiet strength to say, "I can see this clearly without losing
myself in it."

## The Difference Between Reaction and Response

Emotionally attached leaders react.
They take things personally, absorb others' energy, and make decisions
from urgency rather than wisdom.
Their emotional field gets tangled with the team's, and clarity
disappears.

Emotionally intelligent leaders, however, respond.
They pause before they speak. They observe before they intervene.
They trust before they correct.

That pause — that small, conscious space between stimulus and
response — is where detachment lives.
It's not emotional distance; it's emotional maturity in motion.

Detachment is not coldness — it's clarity in motion.

## Emotional Containment vs. Emotional Suppression

Many leaders were taught that professionalism means suppressing emotion — keeping a poker face and "not taking things personally." But suppression isn't strength; it's stagnation.
Suppressed emotion doesn't disappear — it hides, then leaks into tone, tension, or decision-making.

Emotional containment, on the other hand, is conscious energy management.
It's the ability to feel fully but channel emotion constructively.
It's saying: "I can acknowledge this frustration, this excitement, this fear — and still choose how I direct it."

Containment builds credibility because people can feel your steadiness. It creates safety. Teams think, "If my leader can stay calm here, we'll be okay."

## Story: The Executive Who Paused

A senior marketing director once shared how a heated client email triggered her. Her first instinct was to defend the team, write a detailed rebuttal, and "set the record straight."

Instead, she took a 10-minute walk — a self-imposed Pause. Breathe. Reframe. moment.
When she returned, her energy had shifted.
She responded not from defense, but from grounded clarity: "I hear your frustration. Let's regroup and revisit what success looks like together."

The result? The client apologized, renewed the contract, and praised her professionalism.

She later reflected, "That ten-minute pause changed everything. It wasn't silence — it was strategy."

**The Energetic Maturity Curve**

Emotionally intelligent detachment evolves through three stages:

1. **Emotional Reactivity:** Energy moves you. (You absorb and project emotion unconsciously.)

2. **Emotional Awareness:** You notice energy. (You can name what you feel without acting on it.)

3. **Emotional Mastery:** You direct energy. (You hold steady while guiding others into alignment.)

The journey from reactivity to mastery is the evolution of energetic leadership.
You no longer fear emotion — you navigate it.

Emotional maturity is the ability to hold peace in the presence of pressure.

**Energetic Practices for Emotional Detachment**

1. **Pause Practice:** Before reacting to an email, comment, or decision, take three deep breaths. Ask: "What's the most aligned energy I can bring here?"

2. **Energy Audit:** At the end of each day, check your emotional bank. Where did you overspend energy on things beyond your control?

3.  **Reframing Ritual:** Replace "I have to fix this" with "I get to hold space for this." The language of leadership changes the energy of leadership

## Why Detachment Inspires Confidence

Emotionally attached leaders are unpredictable — their mood dictates the culture.
Emotionally intelligent leaders are consistent — their presence regulates the culture.

People don't follow titles; they follow energy stability.
When leaders maintain calm objectivity, it sends a silent but powerful message: "We're safe here."

That safety opens the door to creativity, communication, and connection — the foundations of inspired performance.

Emotionally intelligent detachment is love in leadership form.
It's the ability to hold others through chaos without becoming it.

## Section 4: The Business Impact — When Trust Becomes Strategy

In most organizations, trust is treated like a value — something to aspire to, discuss in meetings, or display on a poster.
But in reality, **trust is a strategy.** It's an invisible operating system that determines how quickly, efficiently, and creatively a company can move.

Detachment is the mechanism that activates that strategy.
Because trust and control cannot coexist — one expands energy, the other restricts it.

When leaders replace control with trust, they set in motion a chain reaction that transforms culture, decision-making, and results.

Trust is not soft. It's scalable.

## The Energetic ROI of Trust

Organizations spend billions on systems designed to enforce accountability, yet the most powerful accountability mechanism in existence is mutual trust.
When people are trusted, they naturally rise to meet that belief.

That's not philosophy — it's neuroscience.
Trust releases oxytocin, the hormone that fosters collaboration, loyalty, and empathy.
It literally changes how the brain perceives challenge — replacing anxiety with possibility.

Teams who feel trusted think faster, recover quicker, and connect deeper.
They stop playing defense and start playing offense — because they're no longer wasting energy proving their worth.

Trust is the ultimate performance enhancer because it aligns human emotion with organizational intention.

When people feel trusted, they stop protecting themselves and start expressing themselves.

## From Control to Confidence

Control creates compliance.
Trust creates commitment.

Control says, "Do this or else."
Trust says, "I believe you'll make the right call."

In a control-based culture, people seek permission.
In a trust-based culture, people seek possibility.

The energy difference between those two worlds determines everything:
speed, innovation, morale, and profit.

It's not that control never works — it's that it doesn't scale.
You can control ten people. You can't control a thousand.
But you can inspire a thousand through trust.

Confidence is more contagious than control.

## Story: The Four-Day Leap

A manufacturing company faced rising turnover and burnout.
Productivity was flat despite mandatory overtime. Leadership decided to experiment with a bold idea: a four-day workweek.

At first, executives resisted — afraid that less time meant less output.
But they agreed to a 90-day pilot based on one principle: trust the people to manage themselves.

By week four, productivity rose by 15%. Employee satisfaction doubled. Absenteeism nearly disappeared.
The team self-organized, communicated better, and delivered faster — because they felt trusted to do so.

When the pilot ended, the company didn't just keep the four-day week — they made "trust as structure" a permanent part of their culture.

## Trust as Time Management

The more you trust, the less you chase.
Leaders who trust their people waste fewer hours checking, redoing, or micromanaging.
That reclaimed time becomes creative capital — energy that can now be invested in innovation, relationships, and vision.

In this way, trust is not only emotional currency — it's operational efficiency.

Trust is the most powerful time management tool in business.

It allows leaders to shift from "How can I control this?" to "Who already has the answer?"
And in that shift, energy moves faster than any process ever could.

## The Invisible Architecture of High-Trust Companies

High-trust organizations have a recognizable energetic signature:

- Meetings are shorter, yet more productive.

- Communication is open, not guarded.

- Innovation happens organically, not by assignment.

- Employees speak truth to leadership without fear.

Customers sense this, too. They feel the authenticity in every interaction. Because when internal energy flows freely, external relationships resonate effortlessly.

Trust becomes the company's frequency — one that naturally attracts alignment, loyalty, and opportunity.

**Energetic Truth**

When trust becomes strategy, business stops being a contest of control and becomes an ecosystem of co-creation.
Energy circulates. People feel safe. Progress compounds.

That's what detachment really creates — the energetic conditions for trust to thrive.

When you stop needing to control outcomes,
outcomes start aligning themselves with your vision.

**Section 5: Manifest This in Your Company — Exercises**

Detachment is not something you achieve once — it's a practice you return to daily.
It's the habit of releasing tension, trusting timing, and leading from energetic calm instead of control.
These exercises are designed to help individuals, teams, and leaders build that muscle — to trade pressure for power and urgency for flow.

**1. The Control Inventory**

**Purpose:** To identify where control has become an unconscious drain on energy.

**How to do it:**

- On a whiteboard or digital document, create two columns: **What I'm trying to control** and **What's actually within my control.**

- List your current projects, decisions, and worries under the first column.

- For each, ask:
  "Do I have direct influence over this, or am I holding tension for something beyond my reach?"

- Move anything outside your direct influence into a "release" list.

**Insight:**
This creates immediate emotional clarity. You'll see that most stress is tied to things you can't control — and that releasing them restores creative energy.

Awareness is the first act of detachment.

## 2. The 24-Hour Release Rule

**Purpose:** To transform reaction into reflection.

**How to do it:**
When a situation triggers emotion — an angry email, a sudden problem, a disappointing result — commit to this practice:

1. **Pause.** No decisions, no responses, no rants for 24 hours.

2. **Breathe.** Allow emotion to settle; energy clears with time.

3. **Revisit.** After 24 hours, ask: "What does this need now — action or perspective?"

### Insight:
Nine times out of ten, you'll respond with greater wisdom and less waste.
Detachment turns urgency into insight.

Reaction creates chaos. Reflection creates clarity.

## 3. Outcome vs. Intention Mapping

**Purpose:** To redirect focus from external metrics to energetic purpose.

**How to do it:**
For each major initiative or goal, write two statements:

- **Outcome:** What do we want to happen?

- **Intention:** Why does it matter?

Then, consciously release the outcome and align your energy to the intention.
The outcome may change — but if the intention stays aligned, success will always take its right form.

### Example:

- Outcome: "Hit $10 million in revenue."

- Intention: "Expand impact by connecting more customers to our vision."

**Insight:**
When you anchor to intention, you're guided by energy, not ego.

Detach from the metric. Attach to the meaning.

### 4. The Surrender Circle

**Purpose:** To strengthen collective trust and energetic release across leadership.

**How to do it:**

- Once a month, gather the leadership team for a 30-minute meeting focused solely on release.

- Each person names one thing they've been holding too tightly — a result, a conflict, a fear.

- As each person shares, the group responds with a single phrase: "We trust this will work out in the right time, in the right way."

You'll feel the room lighten as tension dissolves. The goal isn't problem-solving — it's energetic cleansing.

**Insight:**
Releasing together builds trust together.
A surrendered team becomes a powerful one because energy moves through it freely.

Surrender is not giving up. It's giving over — to wisdom larger than your own.

## 5. The Trust Test

**Purpose:** To rebuild trust through action instead of discussion.

**How to do it:**
Choose one process this month to simplify.
Reduce one approval layer, hand off one decision, or empower one team member to lead without oversight.
Track what happens over 30 days.

You'll likely find that performance doesn't drop — it rises.
Because people always rise to meet belief.

**Insight:**
Detachment at the leadership level becomes empowerment at the employee level.

Every time you trust someone, you multiply their capacity to succeed.

## Energetic Takeaway

Detachment is the quiet discipline of power — the ability to release, allow, and realign without losing focus or faith.
The more you practice it, the faster energy moves, and the more effortless success becomes.

Because when a company collectively lets go of control,
it stops forcing outcomes and starts attracting them.

Letting go is the secret to moving forward.

## Section 6: Reflection Prompts

Detachment begins where awareness deepens.
Before an organization can release control, its people must first recognize where control is holding them.
These prompts are designed to bring that awareness to the surface — to help leaders and teams shift from tension to trust, from gripping to allowing.

### For Leaders

### 1. Where am I confusing control with competence?
Do I believe I'm being responsible by managing every detail — or am I afraid of what might happen if I don't?

### 2. What outcomes am I gripping too tightly?
Are there projects, numbers, or perceptions I've attached my identity to?
What would happen if I trusted that they're already unfolding exactly as they should?

### 3. How do I respond when things don't go to plan?
Do I panic, push harder, or pause and observe?
How might calm detachment actually solve problems faster than intensity ever could?

### 4. Where can I model trust more openly?
Could I delegate a decision, release a report for team ownership, or show vulnerability in a meeting?
Trust multiplies when it's demonstrated, not demanded.

### 5. Am I creating space for others to rise?
When I let go, do I leave room for others to grow — or do I rush in to "fix" things that aren't mine to fix?

Leadership without control isn't weakness — it's wisdom in motion.

**For Teams**

**1. Do I trust leadership's vision, even when I can't see every step?**
If not, what would help me feel more confident in the direction we're headed?

**2. Where do I still need external approval before I act?**
Is that because of culture, habit, or fear?
How could I reclaim my creative confidence?

**3. What's one outcome I can emotionally detach from this week?**
Can I focus on the intention — doing meaningful work — instead of obsessing over the result?

**4. How does letting go feel in my body?**
Does it bring peace or discomfort?
If it feels unsettling, what story am I telling myself about control and safety?

**5. When was the last time I allowed something to unfold — and it worked out even better than expected?**
Revisit that memory.
It's proof that trust is not passive — it's powerful.

When you trust the process, the process begins to trust you.

**Team Reflection Practice: The Trust Pulse**

Once per week, invite your team into a five-minute "Trust Pulse" check-in.
Ask one question:

"Where can we replace tension with trust this week?"

Allow open, honest sharing — even if it's small things.
Maybe it's trusting a new system, a new leader, or simply the timing of a project.
Each act of awareness is a release point.

When you consistently take the pulse of trust, you create a living rhythm of detachment — one that breathes energy back into the culture.

## Energetic Reflection

The more you trust, the more energy becomes available for creation.
The less you grip, the more naturally success unfolds.
Detachment is how organizations move from survival to expansion — not through control, but through confidence in the unseen.

Letting go isn't losing power — it's remembering where true power comes from.

## Section 7: Closing Affirmation

There is a sacred stillness that follows surrender.
It's the silence after effort — the moment when you've given your best, and you simply allow life, timing, and the intelligence of the whole to take over.

That stillness is not empty.
It's alive with unseen coordination.
It's the hum of alignment at work behind the scenes.

Detachment is not about giving up control — it's about releasing resistance.
It's the understanding that what is meant for you, your team, your company, cannot be missed.

When leaders and organizations embody this truth, their energy changes.
They stop chasing what's next and start magnetizing what's right.
Meetings become calmer. Decisions become clearer. Progress feels lighter.

The paradox of power is that the more you relax into trust, the faster results find you.
The more you detach from needing outcomes, the more outcomes align effortlessly.

Because the universe — and business — respond to energy, not effort.
And energy flows where tension ends.

**Detachment is the highest form of faith.**
**It's where action becomes effortless,**
**and excellence becomes inevitable.**

So breathe.
Trust your vision.
Release what's not yours to hold.

And remember — what's aligned with you will always arrive on time.

# Chapter 6 — Identity Alignment: Becoming the Brand You Believe In

## Section 1: The Power of Identity Alignment

"When who you are matches what you say — trust, culture, and success align effortlessly."

Every organization has an energy — a vibration that's felt long before it's seen.
You can sense it the moment you walk into a company's office, attend its meeting, or interact with its brand.
That energy is identity in motion.

Identity alignment is what happens when a company's inner world — its beliefs, values, and intentions — matches its outer expression — its actions, products, and communication.
It's the moment when message and behavior harmonize.
When the brand doesn't just speak its truth — it lives it.

Authenticity is the new strategy.

### The Energy of Congruence

In a misaligned company, there's always friction.
The marketing says one thing, but the culture says another.
The mission statement promises innovation, but the meetings breed fear.
The website shines with "purpose," but employees whisper exhaustion.

That energetic mismatch creates dissonance — the invisible static that people can feel even if they can't explain it.
Customers sense it. Partners hesitate. Employees disengage.

But when energy and action align, something remarkable happens.
The company begins to resonate.
Every message feels believable, every interaction feels real.
People trust what they can feel, not what they're told.

Identity alignment, therefore, isn't just brand consistency — it's energetic integrity.

Alignment builds trust faster than marketing ever could.

## When the Inside Matches the Outside

The most magnetic companies aren't the ones that advertise the loudest — they're the ones that live the clearest.
Their inner truth and outer image are indistinguishable.

You see it in how their teams speak, how their leaders behave, how their customers feel.
Everything reflects a unified vibration — calm, confident, and coherent.

A luxury brand that truly values craftsmanship doesn't need to explain quality — you can feel it in every detail.
A company that believes in empowerment doesn't need slogans — you see it in how employees make decisions.

This coherence is what customers call "authenticity," but energetically it's alignment.
It's the same principle that governs human relationships: when words and actions match, trust deepens instantly.

## Story: The Company That Realigned Instead of Rebranding

A technology firm was struggling with public perception. Their marketing promised simplicity and connection, yet internally they were siloed, rigid, and burned out.
Leadership initially planned a full rebrand — new logo, new message, new campaign.

But one consultant asked a simple question:

"Before you change your message, why not live it first?"

That question shifted everything.
Instead of rebranding, they realigned.
Departments began collaborating openly. Meetings shortened. Leaders simplified internal communication.
Six months later, they didn't just have a new look — they had a new frequency.

When the internal energy changed, the external perception followed.
The rebrand they thought they needed became unnecessary.

You don't fix brand problems — you fix energy problems.

## Identity as Frequency

Every company is a frequency broadcast.
Your culture emits it, your customers receive it, and the world responds accordingly.
When the message and the vibration don't match, the signal weakens.
When they do match, the company becomes magnetic.

Identity alignment means that the company's external story and internal truth vibrate at the same pitch.
That's when branding becomes effortless, retention increases, and success compounds.

Because people don't just follow companies — they follow congruence.
They trust what feels right.

Authenticity doesn't attract everyone — it attracts the right ones.

## Energetic Summary

Identity alignment is not about creating an image — it's about embodying one.
It's what happens when vision turns into vibration, and values become visible.
It's how a company stops marketing who it wants to be and starts living who it really is.

True branding is the art of being — not performing.

When identity aligns, energy amplifies — and the world feels it.

## Section 2: Culture as the Living Brand

Every brand has two versions of itself:
the one it markets — and the one it lives.

The lived version is culture.
It's the collective energy of how people treat one another, how decisions are made, and how values are expressed when no one is watching.

Culture is the mirror that reflects whether your brand identity is real or rehearsed.
You can't design culture in a meeting — you transmit it through behavior, tone, and energy every single day.

Brand is not what you say. It's how your people make others feel.

## Culture as Energy in Motion

Culture is not a static set of values on a wall — it's energy in motion.
It's the vibration created by thousands of micro-interactions:
how leaders respond to mistakes, how teams handle pressure, how wins are celebrated, how challenges are framed.

Each choice either reinforces the brand or erodes it.

When culture and brand are aligned, the energy is coherent.
Every interaction, from a customer call to an internal email, carries the same signature: trust, clarity, confidence, authenticity.
People inside the company feel it — and people outside experience it.

Culture is your brand in its most human form.

## The Internal → External Loop

Culture is the seed; brand is the bloom.
What grows externally in the market always mirrors what's planted internally.

If employees feel unseen, customers will too.
If teams feel empowered, clients will sense that empowerment in the
service they receive.
If leaders operate from fear, it will ripple into the tone of every
communication.

Energy doesn't lie — it leaks.
You can't brand your way around energetic misalignment.

This is why culture is the real marketing department.
It determines whether your message resonates or rings hollow.

You can't fake frequency. People feel what's real.

## Story: The Hospitality Brand That Shifted from Policy to Presence

A boutique hotel chain noticed declining guest reviews despite
significant investment in advertising and property upgrades. The issue
wasn't service — it was spirit.

Employees followed every procedure perfectly, yet interactions felt
mechanical. The hotel promised warmth, but guests felt formality.

Leadership made a pivotal shift: they removed rigid scripts and
encouraged staff to connect authentically — to smile, remember
names, and share small personal touches.

Within three months, reviews skyrocketed. Not one new ad campaign,
not one new renovation — just a cultural re-alignment toward presence
over policy.

Their energy became their marketing.

Culture is how your brand breathes through people.

## Culture as Brand Transmission

Employees are not brand ambassadors because of title — they're brand transmitters because of energy.
Every conversation, email, or client interaction carries a frequency.

When that frequency matches the company's purpose and promise, people feel it immediately.
They don't just experience the brand — they experience its truth.

A company with aligned culture doesn't need to "train" employees to represent the brand. They embody it. It becomes instinct, not instruction.

The most powerful brand training is energetic coherence.

## The Culture Feedback Loop

Culture feeds brand, and brand feeds culture.
When employees see customers respond positively to authenticity, they're encouraged to bring more of it.
When they see leadership model integrity, they mirror it in their own behavior.
The loop strengthens with every act of alignment.

Culture is a living system — it evolves through energy exchange.
The healthier the energy, the stronger the brand's pulse.

When the inside vibrates higher, the outside shines brighter.

**Energetic Summary**

Culture is your brand's heartbeat — the steady rhythm that gives everything else life.
Logos, taglines, and campaigns may express your message, but culture expresses your soul.

A company becomes unstoppable when its internal energy (how it lives) matches its external image (how it's seen).
That is identity alignment in its purest form.

Culture isn't built by intention alone — it's built by vibration.

When you raise the frequency within, the brand begins to radiate effortlessly.

## Section 3: Leadership Identity — Walking the Talk

Every company is a reflection of its leadership frequency.
Culture doesn't begin in the break room — it begins in the boardroom.

The way leaders show up — their tone, decisions, body language, and beliefs — sets the energetic ceiling for everyone else.
Employees don't align with what leaders say; they align with what leaders embody.

Leadership identity sets the frequency for the entire brand.

## The Mirror Effect

The team mirrors the leader. Always.
If leadership is anxious, the culture hums with tension.
If leadership is grounded, the company breathes with calm.
If leadership is inspired, teams create from inspiration.

This mirroring is energetic, not procedural.
You can't tell people to "believe in the vision" if you don't vibrate belief yourself.
You can't expect innovation when you lead from fear.

Authenticity cascades downward.
The leader's energy becomes the company's emotional climate.

People don't follow words — they follow vibration.

## Energetic Integrity

Energetic integrity means your inner state and outer expression are aligned.
It's when what you believe, say, and do all move in the same direction.

When a leader says "We value people first," but cuts corners on employee well-being, that vibration of contradiction ripples instantly through the organization.
Energy reads faster than words.

But when a leader consistently embodies the values they promote — transparency, empathy, excellence — trust becomes automatic.
People relax. Communication opens. The organization starts operating from coherence rather than confusion.

Integrity is not just moral — it's magnetic.

## Story: The Leader Who Became the Brand

A mid-size marketing agency was struggling with retention. Leadership preached creativity, yet employees felt constrained by bureaucracy and fear of failure.

Then, the CEO made one radical decision: to live the brand.
He stopped approving every campaign. He encouraged risk-taking and publicly celebrated "creative misfires" as learning moments.

Soon, employees started experimenting again.
Energy shifted.
Clients noticed.

The agency's tagline — "Create Fearlessly" — stopped being a slogan and became a lived experience.

Six months later, their retention rate rose 40%. Not because of incentives or perks — but because the CEO finally embodied the identity he'd been selling.

When leaders live the message, the message becomes movement.

## Authenticity in Action

Authenticity doesn't mean oversharing — it means operating without energetic disguise.
It's leading with transparency, even when the truth is uncomfortable.
It's saying, "I don't have all the answers," but radiating confidence that the team will find them together.

The more authentic a leader becomes, the more permission others feel to show up authentically too.
And authenticity is contagious — it multiplies across teams, departments, and eventually, the brand itself.

Authentic leaders don't need authority — their energy carries it.

**The Leadership Alignment Formula**

1. **Clarity:** Know what you stand for.

2. **Consistency:** Model it every day.

3. **Congruence:** Ensure your energy, actions, and words align.

When these three align, leadership becomes an energetic transmission. It no longer has to command — it attracts.

**Energetic Leadership Practices**

- **Energetic Check-In:** Before entering a meeting, pause and ask, "What frequency am I bringing into this room?"

- **Micro-Integrity Moments:** When small ethical or emotional decisions arise, choose alignment over comfort.

- **Authenticity Amplifiers:** Share the why behind decisions — not just the what. It turns compliance into connection.

The most inspiring leaders are not performers — they're permission givers.

**Energetic Summary**

When leadership identity and company identity align, everything flows faster: communication, innovation, morale, and trust.
The brand begins to speak with one clear voice — not through marketing, but through modeling.

The world doesn't need more slogans; it needs more leaders who embody their truth.

When leaders walk the talk, alignment becomes automatic.

## Section 4: The Business Impact — Authenticity as Currency

In a noisy world filled with brands shouting for attention, authenticity has become the rarest — and most valuable — currency.
It can't be manufactured, outsourced, or automated.
It's earned through energetic consistency — when who you say you are and how you actually show up feel like the same thing.

That congruence creates instant trust.
And trust, in business, is conversion.

The most profitable brands are energetically congruent.

### Authenticity as an Economic Advantage

Authenticity isn't just a feel-good concept — it's a growth strategy.
Companies that operate from genuine alignment with their purpose outperform those that don't, across every measurable metric:

- **Customer loyalty** — repeat buyers are drawn to real energy.

- **Employee retention** — people stay where they can be authentic.

- **Brand advocacy** — aligned customers become evangelists, not just consumers.

Because authenticity lowers resistance.
It eliminates friction between marketing and delivery, promise and performance, leadership and culture.
That frictionless energy translates directly into efficiency — both emotional and financial.

Authenticity reduces the energy cost of doing business.

## The Hidden Cost of Inauthenticity

Misalignment is expensive.
When the brand says one thing but the behavior says another, the organization spends enormous energy managing perception.
That's marketing money trying to fix a vibration problem.

You can't buy trust. You become it.
And the cost of pretending is burnout — for both the company and the customer.

Employees who have to perform values they don't feel eventually disengage.
Customers who sense inconsistency subconsciously pull away.
The result is energetic leakage — lost trust, lost clarity, lost revenue.

When energy and message diverge, the market always feels it first.

**Story: The Authentic Pivot**

A national retailer once faced public backlash for overpromising sustainability without real proof. Their PR team scrambled to repair the narrative — until the CEO made a bold move: he admitted the gap.

He issued a letter to customers saying,

"We spoke before we were fully ready to live it. Now, we're building systems that match our words."

The letter went viral — not because it was perfect, but because it was real.
Sales dipped briefly, then recovered stronger than before. Employees felt proud again. Investors responded with renewed confidence.

The company didn't lose credibility — it gained humanity.

Transparency is the new loyalty program.

**Authenticity in the Age of Automation**

In an era where technology can replicate almost anything — voices, faces, even emotions — authenticity becomes priceless.
It's the one thing that can't be faked, coded, or copied.

Your energy is your differentiation.
Your honesty is your advantage.

Consumers are becoming energetic readers — they can feel whether a brand is aligned or performing.
They don't just buy products; they buy frequency.

In the future of business, energy is the new marketing.

## Energetic Branding = Ease

When your brand and identity are aligned, business becomes energetically efficient.

- You no longer need to "sell" — people resonate naturally.

- You no longer need constant rebranding — you evolve organically.

- You no longer burn out — because your energy and your message move in the same direction.

Authenticity removes resistance.
It allows the company's energy to flow unobstructed — from vision to voice to value.

When energy is aligned, momentum is automatic.

## The Tangible ROI of Alignment

Studies show that purpose-driven, authentic companies:

- Achieve 40% higher engagement rates.

- Experience up to 3x higher customer lifetime value.

- Recover faster from market crises.

But beyond statistics, there's an unquantifiable truth:
Aligned companies feel better to work for, buy from, and collaborate with.

That feeling becomes the brand's greatest asset — one that no competitor can replicate.

Authenticity creates belonging — and belonging is the strongest retention tool in existence.

## Energetic Summary

Authenticity is the intersection of truth and trust.
It's the moment when alignment becomes visible, measurable, and magnetic.
In business, as in life, people don't follow perfection — they follow presence.

Authenticity isn't a differentiator anymore. It's the baseline for trust.

When energy, action, and identity match, you don't have to convince anyone you're real.
They can feel it.

## Section 5: Manifest This in Your Company — Exercises

Identity alignment isn't a one-time calibration — it's a continuous practice of matching vibration to vision.
The following exercises are designed to help you reconnect with your company's truth, refine how it's expressed, and close the gap between what you say and what you actually radiate.

## 1. The Identity Audit

**Purpose:** To uncover where internal culture and external brand may be out of sync.

**How to do it:**
Gather a cross-functional team and create three lists:

- **What we say we are.** (Your brand statements, mission, tagline.)

- **What we actually are.** (Behaviors, energy, culture as employees experience it.)

- **What we want to be.** (Your aligned future state.)

Compare the three. Highlight where energy and action don't match the message.
These are not failures — they're recalibration points.

**Insight:**
Every misalignment is simply a place where intention needs to meet embodiment.

Your brand promise means nothing until your energy keeps it.

## 2. The Energy Check

**Purpose:** To ensure that your customer experience feels like your mission statement sounds.

**How to do it:**

- Choose one touchpoint: onboarding call, showroom visit, email, or website interaction.

- Experience it as a customer would.

- Ask: "Does this interaction carry the emotion, tone, and energy our brand stands for?"

If your mission says "connection," does your communication feel warm and personal?
If your brand says "innovation," does your process feel modern and intuitive?

**Insight:**
Brand isn't about words — it's about the emotional frequency of every touchpoint.

When energy matches message, customers don't need convincing — they just feel right.

## 3. The Brand Mirror Exercise

**Purpose:** To measure internal perception versus external projection.

**How to do it:**
Invite employees to describe the brand in their own words. Ask:

- "What does our company stand for?"

- "How do we make people feel?"

- "What do we do better than anyone else?"

Compare their answers to your official brand statements and marketing materials.
If the language doesn't match, neither does the energy.

**Insight:**
Your employees are the brand.
When they speak in harmony, your message resonates louder than any ad campaign could.

When people speak the same truth, they broadcast the same frequency.

## 4. The Alignment Manifesto

**Purpose:** To rewrite your company's identity through the lens of authenticity.

**How to do it:**

- Review your mission, vision, and value statements.

- Circle every phrase that feels outdated, performative, or disconnected.

- Rewrite each one using emotional truth — language that feels real, not rehearsed.

Example:
Before: "We strive for excellence in customer service."
After: "We care deeply about every person we serve — because we believe business is built on relationships."

Display your new "Alignment Manifesto" where everyone can feel it.

**Insight:**
When your language speaks from the heart, your culture follows suit.

Words aligned with energy become truth in action.

## 5. The Leadership Reflection Loop

**Purpose:** To ensure alignment begins where it matters most — at the top.

**How to do it:**
Each week, leaders reflect on these three questions:

1. "Did my energy this week reflect the brand I represent?"

2. "Where did I speak values but fail to live them?"

3. "What's one behavior I can adjust to re-align with our truth?"

When leaders model realignment, employees mirror it naturally. Authenticity starts as a personal discipline before it becomes an organizational one.

**Insight:**
Culture doesn't change through mandates — it changes through mirrors.

When leaders recalibrate their energy, the whole organization vibrates higher.

## Energetic Takeaway

Identity alignment is the bridge between intention and impact.
It's how energy becomes brand, and brand becomes trust.

When the message, the mission, and the emotion all flow in one direction, the company moves from being seen to being felt.

Your identity is not your logo — it's your frequency.

And when that frequency is honest, the world can't help but believe.

## Section 6: Reflection Prompts

Identity alignment starts with awareness.
It asks every person in an organization to look beyond titles and tactics — to explore whether the energy they bring each day reflects the truth of who they (and the company) say they are.

Use these prompts as mirrors — gentle, revealing, and transformative.

## For Leaders

### 1. Does my leadership energy match our company's message?
If we say we value creativity, do I lead with curiosity or control?
If we promote innovation, do I create safety for risk-taking — or fear of mistakes?

### 2. What part of our brand identity feels authentic, and what feels aspirational?
Am I trying to prove something, or embody something?
Where might our marketing be outpacing our maturity?

### 3. How do I respond when someone challenges "the way we've always done it"?

Do I defend the brand, or invite evolution?
Detachment from the old allows identity to grow.

### 4. When was the last time I visibly lived one of our values?

Did people see me lead through empathy, integrity, or openness — or did I talk about it instead?

### 5. What energy do I leave behind in meetings, emails, and decisions?

Is it aligned with our mission, or does it contradict it?
Leaders are energetic broadcasters — everything they emit becomes part of the brand's vibration.

Leadership alignment isn't about perfection — it's about congruence.

### For Teams

### 1. When I describe our company to friends or family, what energy comes through?

Does it sound proud, inspired, uncertain, or detached?
That feeling reveals how aligned you are with the brand's frequency.

### 2. Do I believe in what we say publicly?

If not, what part feels off — and what truth needs to be voiced?
Alignment can't exist where silence protects disconnection.

### 3. What behaviors or traditions in our workplace feel outdated or performative?

Are there rituals we've outgrown that keep us stuck in an old identity?

## 4. How do I personally embody our brand values?

If our brand stands for trust, creativity, or care — how do I express that in my own work?

## 5. Where do I feel most in flow at work — and what makes that possible?

Flow always reveals alignment.
Pay attention to where energy feels natural — that's your personal brand frequency connecting to the company's.

When employees align with the company's truth, their work becomes transmission.

## Collective Team Reflection

At your next team meeting, ask this single question:

"If our company were a person, would its actions match its words?"

Invite open, non-judgmental dialogue.
The goal isn't to critique but to listen — to identify energetic dissonance and commit to restoring harmony.

The discussion itself is a realignment practice.
When truth is spoken collectively, energy begins to recalibrate instantly.

## Energetic Reflection

Identity alignment is about honesty — the courage to look at what's real instead of what's rehearsed.
When you bring integrity into awareness, transformation begins naturally.

Every time you align intention with action, emotion with mission, and leadership with truth, you raise the company's energetic frequency — and with it, its impact.

Alignment is not what you declare — it's what you demonstrate.

## Section 7: Closing Affirmation

There is a quiet confidence that comes from being aligned —
from knowing that what you say and what you do are no longer separate,
that your energy and your message speak the same language.

Alignment doesn't shout.
It doesn't have to.
Its power is in its coherence —
in the calm certainty that truth, when lived, always attracts what's meant for it.

When companies reach this state, their brand stops being something they manage
and becomes something they embody.
Their words stop selling and start resonating.
Their culture stops performing and starts breathing.

Because alignment is magnetic.
It pulls opportunity, talent, and trust into its orbit without needing to chase them.
People recognize something real when they feel it —
and realness is the rarest currency of all.

**Identity alignment is where words become truth,
and truth becomes power.**

When who you are matches what you promise,
there is no resistance, no dissonance, no confusion.
Only flow.

That is the true secret of influence —
not performance, but presence.
Not image, but integrity.

To be aligned is to be trusted.
To be trusted is to be chosen.
And to be chosen, again and again,
is what turns energy into empire.

# Chapter 7 — Overcoming Resistance: The Hidden Energies that Hold Companies Back

## Section 1: Understanding Resistance as Energy

"What you resist, persists — in business, in culture, and in energy."

Resistance is often misunderstood.
Most leaders view it as an obstacle to overcome — a problem to fix, a person to persuade, a delay to manage.
But resistance isn't an enemy; it's information.

In energetic terms, resistance is simply the body of a company saying, "Something here needs attention."
It's communication, not confrontation.

Resistance shows up when energy wants to move forward — but something old, afraid, or unaligned is holding it back.
And the moment you stop fighting resistance and start listening to it, it becomes the roadmap to growth.

Resistance isn't opposition — it's communication.

## The Language of Resistance

Resistance speaks in symptoms.
In organizations, it rarely announces itself directly. Instead, it whispers through patterns:

- Endless meetings without movement.

- Excuses disguised as "process."

- Turnover that repeats in the same department.

- Innovation that never seems to make it past discussion.

- Energy that feels heavy, tense, or fragmented.

These are not just management issues — they're energetic feedback loops.
Each one reveals where flow has been blocked, where fear has replaced trust, or where clarity has faded into confusion.

Once you learn to interpret these signals, resistance stops being frustrating — it becomes diagnostic.

What feels like friction is often transformation trying to happen.

## How Resistance Manifests

At its core, resistance is fear of expansion.
It's the ego of the organization — the part that wants progress, but also safety.
The part that says, "Let's grow," while secretly whispering, "But not too much."

This tension plays out in subtle ways:

- **In leaders:** resistance shows as overcontrol, perfectionism, or constant busyness.

- **In teams:** it appears as disengagement, passive compliance, or surface-level collaboration.

- **In culture:** it becomes bureaucracy, silos, or cynicism disguised as professionalism.

But underneath all of it is the same truth — a company can't expand past what it's willing to energetically release.

## Story: The Company That Mistook Conflict for Crisis

A home design firm noticed a growing divide between its creative and operations teams. Meetings felt tense, collaboration was breaking down, and leadership began labeling it a "communication problem."

But the real issue wasn't communication — it was resistance.
The creative team was evolving faster than the company's old systems could support, and the friction was the sound of growth.

Once leadership stopped trying to fix the conflict and instead asked, "What truth is this tension trying to reveal?" — everything shifted.

They discovered outdated approval processes, unspoken resentments, and a collective fear of change.
By naming those energies and aligning around trust, the same tension that once felt like chaos became the catalyst for innovation.

Resistance was never the problem — denial was.

## The Energetics of Movement

Energy always seeks flow.
When it meets resistance, it pauses, builds pressure, and waits for permission to move again.
That buildup can feel uncomfortable — but it's not negative. It's potential energy waiting for direction.

In companies, that means resistance is the sign that evolution is already underway.
The key is not to suppress it, but to channel it.

When leaders meet resistance with curiosity instead of control, the energy behind it transforms into momentum.
The very friction that once slowed progress becomes the spark that accelerates it.

Every moment of resistance is an invitation to realignment.

Energetic Summary

Resistance is not proof that you're off track — it's proof that you're growing.
It's the stretch between the current vibration and the next level of expansion.
And when a company learns to interpret resistance as data — not danger — it becomes unstoppable.

What you resist, persists.
What you acknowledge, transforms.

## Section 2: The Psychology of Organizational Fear

Fear is the root of all resistance.
It's the invisible current that runs beneath tension, stagnation, and control.
And in business, fear rarely calls itself by name — it disguises itself as structure, caution, or "best practice."

Fear disguises itself as logic. But intuition knows the truth.

## The Subtle Masks of Fear

In most organizations, fear wears a professional face.
It looks responsible, careful, even strategic.
But if you listen closely, you'll hear its real voice beneath the surface.

- "We can't change that yet" often means "I'm afraid of losing control."

- "That's too risky" often means "I don't trust myself to handle what comes next."

- "Let's wait for more data" often means "I don't want to make the wrong move."

Fear always sounds rational. That's what makes it so powerful — and so sneaky.

When fear takes root in a company, it becomes the silent architect of resistance.
It builds systems to avoid mistakes instead of encouraging discovery.
It values predictability over creativity.
And slowly, without meaning to, the organization trades evolution for comfort.

Fear builds fences where innovation needs space.

## How Fear Infects Culture

Fear spreads energetically.
It travels through tone, body language, and silence.
When a leader operates from anxiety — even unconsciously — that vibration ripples through the organization.

People begin to censor themselves.
They default to "safe" answers.
They overthink every move.
And before long, what was once a culture of possibility becomes a culture of permission.

No one notices it at first, because fear is quiet.
It doesn't shout — it constricts.
It tightens timelines, lowers creative risk, and limits emotional expression.

Soon, teams are busy — but not bold. Productive — but not inspired. That's what fear does: it replaces flow with friction and calls it "efficiency."

Fear doesn't just slow you down — it changes your frequency.

**The Fear-Trust Continuum**

Every company operates somewhere between two energetic poles: **Fear** and **Trust.**

## Fear-Based Energy  Trust-Based Energy

| Fear-Based Energy | Trust-Based Energy |
|---|---|
| Control | Confidence |
| Secrecy | Transparency |
| Perfectionism | Progress |
| Urgency | Flow |
| Compliance | Creativity |
| Protection | Expansion |

Fear shrinks. Trust expands.
And every leadership decision, every meeting, every interaction moves the company closer to one side or the other.

A single act of trust — giving someone creative autonomy, sharing information transparently, admitting uncertainty — has the power to shift the vibration of an entire department.

Fear controls outcomes. Trust co-creates them.

**Story: The Fear Audit**

A mid-size construction company noticed a pattern: talented employees weren't speaking up. Meetings were quiet, innovation stalled, and turnover was rising.

Leadership assumed it was burnout. But after a private survey, the truth emerged: employees were afraid of being "wrong." The company's perfectionist culture had created emotional risk — failure felt unsafe.

Instead of another training, the CEO held an open "Fear Audit." Every leader shared something they personally feared — from losing credibility to making bad calls. The honesty broke the spell.

That meeting became a monthly ritual. Vulnerability spread faster than fear ever had. Creativity returned.

The company didn't need new policies — it needed a new frequency.

Once fear is spoken, it loses power.

**The Leader's Role in Transforming Fear**

Fear can't be managed — it must be met.
It dissolves in environments of empathy and truth.
When leaders name fear without judgment, they give others permission to do the same.

This is emotional transparency in action:

- Admitting when you don't know.

- Asking for input instead of pretending to have all the answers.

- Creating safety for others to express doubt without repercussion.

The paradox of power is that vulnerability strengthens it.
When leaders lead with trust, teams return that trust with courage.

Vulnerability isn't weakness — it's energetic strength.

## Energetic Summary

Organizational fear is the shadow of potential — the energy that appears right before a breakthrough.
It's the tension between safety and expansion, certainty and creativity.

When companies bring fear into awareness, they don't collapse — they evolve.
Because once you see fear clearly, you can finally choose something higher: trust.

Every time you choose trust over fear, the company's vibration rises.

## Section 3: The Energetic Forms of Resistance

Resistance doesn't always look like rebellion.
Sometimes it hides behind logic, politeness, or even professionalism.
It's the subtle "yes" that really means "no," the quiet tension in a meeting, the delayed decision that no one can quite explain.

Every time energy gets stuck in an organization, resistance is present in one of three forms: **cognitive, emotional, or energetic.**
Each has its own message — and its own remedy.

Every block is just energy asking to move.

# 1. Cognitive Resistance — The Mind's Attachment to the Old

This is the most visible form of resistance — when the intellect clings to what it already knows.
It sounds like:

- "That's not how we've done it before."

- "We tried that once; it didn't work."

- "That's not realistic for our industry."

Cognitive resistance lives in the part of the organization that wants safety through certainty.
It's the ego of the intellect — loyal to what's familiar, suspicious of what's new.

But innovation can't exist where certainty rules.
The solution isn't to fight the logic — it's to expand it.

**How to shift it:**

- Introduce new perspectives without attacking the old ones.

- Replace statements with questions: "What would need to be true for this to work?"

- Celebrate curiosity as competence.

When the mind feels safe to explore, resistance transforms into intelligence.

You don't have to destroy the old system — just loosen its certainty.

## 2. Emotional Resistance — The Heart's Fear of Change

Emotional resistance is quieter but more powerful.
It's the undercurrent of hesitation, the unspoken worry that change means loss.

It sounds like:

- "I'm worried this will overwhelm my team."

- "I don't know if I'm ready for that level of responsibility."

- "I just don't feel good about this direction."

Emotionally resistant energy is rarely about the change itself — it's about the feelings the change evokes: fear, inadequacy, grief, or uncertainty.

**How to shift it:**

- Create emotional permission. Let people express resistance without judgment.

- Listen for what's beneath the words — is it fear of failure, loss of control, or not being seen?

- Replace pressure with empathy.

When emotion feels seen, it relaxes.
And when emotion relaxes, energy flows again.

Emotional resistance dissolves in the presence of understanding.

## 3. Energetic Resistance — The Vibration of Misalignment

This is the most subtle and the most powerful form of resistance.
It's when the company's words and its vibration don't match.

You can feel it in an email that sounds enthusiastic but carries tension,
or a strategy session where everyone agrees but the energy feels flat.
It's the invisible mismatch between what's being said and what's
actually being felt.

Energetic resistance is not personal — it's collective.
It's the company's frequency asking for recalibration.

**How to shift it:**

- Pause instead of pushing. Let the energy settle before taking
  action.

- Revisit the "why" — clarity restores flow faster than force.

- Realign the conversation to authenticity: "Does this feel true to
  us?"

When truth returns, resistance leaves.

Energetic resistance is just the body of the organization asking to
breathe.

## Story: The Meeting That Stopped Itself

A real estate company's leadership team was in the middle of a strategic
planning session that felt strangely off. The agenda was clear, the goals
were smart, but the energy was heavy — unfocused, disconnected.

One leader finally said, "Does anyone else feel like we're pushing too hard?"
Everyone exhaled — literally.

They realized they'd been forcing a direction that no one truly believed in. The next hour wasn't spent revising slides; it was spent realigning on what felt right.

By the end of the meeting, the new plan flowed easily — faster, lighter, more alive.

That's the difference between forcing outcomes and following energy.

When you stop pushing, clarity rushes in.

**How to Read Resistance Energetically**

Ask three questions whenever energy feels stuck:

1. **Is this a mindset issue (cognitive)?** → Expand perspective.

2. **Is this an emotional issue (empathic)?** → Create safety.

3. **Is this an energetic issue (vibrational)?** → Realign truth.

Resistance is not random — it's precise feedback.
It always tells you where energy is being held and how it wants to move.

**Energetic Summary**

Cognitive resistance wants certainty.
Emotional resistance wants safety.
Energetic resistance wants truth.

When you meet each of these needs consciously, resistance dissolves and energy flows.
That's when innovation, morale, and results accelerate — naturally, without force.

You don't fight resistance. You listen to it — until it becomes movement.

## Section 4: The Business Impact — When Resistance Runs the Company

Resistance always costs something.
Even when it's invisible, it creates drag — on time, creativity, morale, and money.
It slows communication, limits innovation, and keeps the company orbiting around the same problems, mistaking motion for momentum.

When resistance runs the company, progress becomes performance — busy but not effective, active but not aligned.
The organization is moving, but not evolving.

Unresolved energy becomes expense.

## Energetic Debt

Just as financial debt accumulates interest, energetic debt accrues every time tension goes unaddressed.
Each avoided conversation, delayed decision, or ignored truth compounds over time — until the cost is no longer sustainable.

Energetic debt shows up as:

- Overstaffing to cover inefficiency.

- Frequent turnover from emotional exhaustion.

- Declining innovation because employees are too drained to imagine.

- Endless "change initiatives" that never actually change anything.

The company begins to pay in burnout, bandwidth, and belief.

And the longer resistance goes unnamed, the heavier it becomes.

Energetic debt is the hidden tax on growth.

## When Fear Becomes the Business Model

Some companies run entirely on resistance energy — the illusion of control, urgency, and constant reactivity.
They mistake stress for productivity and pressure for progress.

Meetings are filled with fire drills. Emails feel urgent but lack meaning.
Employees hustle to meet metrics that no longer reflect purpose.

Over time, this resistance-based operating system becomes normalized. People forget what flow feels like.
They assume exhaustion is the cost of excellence.

But that's not excellence — it's energetic imbalance.

When resistance leads, creativity leaves.

**Story: The Team Running on Resistance**

A national homebuilding company had strong sales but rising turnover. Teams described their days as "constant triage." Leadership was proud of their speed — until a culture audit revealed a deeper truth: employees weren't moving fast because they were inspired; they were moving fast because they were afraid to slow down.

Every mistake felt like a threat. Every pause felt dangerous.
The company's high performance was actually resistance — fear of failure disguised as drive.

Once leadership recognized this, they shifted focus from urgency to trust. Meetings shortened, priorities simplified, and space was created for creative thinking.

Within six months, turnover dropped by 30%. The same people, same systems — just less resistance.

They didn't fix the business. They freed the energy.

## How Resistance Shrinks Possibility

Resistance limits what an organization can even imagine.
It narrows creative thinking, replacing "What if?" with "What could go wrong?"
It makes success conditional — tied to control instead of connection.

This energetic constriction not only drains innovation; it drains joy.
And when joy leaves the building, so does loyalty.

Because people don't leave companies — they leave frequencies.
They leave the vibration of tension, fear, and stagnation in search of places that feel lighter.

Resistance repels both talent and opportunity.

## Breaking the Resistance Cycle

The moment leaders decide to stop running on resistance energy, everything changes.
It begins with a pause — a willingness to stop pushing and ask, "Where are we holding on too tightly?"

That simple awareness begins to dissolve energetic debt.
Communication opens, collaboration returns, and momentum rebuilds — this time from alignment, not anxiety.

The company doesn't just move faster; it moves freer.

You can't scale resistance. You can only release it.

## Energetic Summary

When resistance runs the company, energy is consumed faster than it's replenished.
But when awareness enters, resistance transforms into wisdom.

The cost of unaddressed tension is high — but the return on released energy is exponential.

Every ounce of resistance you release returns as clarity, creativity, and cash flow.

That's not metaphor — it's energetic math.

## Section 5: Manifest This in Your Company — Exercises

Resistance can't be removed by force — it must be released through awareness.
When a company learns to see resistance as energy instead of error, it transforms from reactive to responsive, from defensive to dynamic.

These practices help you translate tension into information, and information into movement.

### 1. The Resistance Map

**Purpose:** To locate where energy feels heavy, slow, or constricted.

**How to do it:**

- Draw a simple map of your organization — departments, teams, or key processes.

- In a group setting, have participants color-code or rate each area:

    o Green = flow

    o Yellow = occasional tension

    o Red = consistent resistance

Then, discuss patterns.
Where are the red zones? What conversations or changes tend to stall there?
Ask: "What's the story this energy is trying to tell us?"

**Insight:**
Patterns reveal the truth before people do. Resistance always gathers where energy isn't being acknowledged.

Resistance hides in the same places we avoid looking.

## 2. The Fear Inquiry

**Purpose:** To uncover the emotion beneath recurring roadblocks.

**How to do it:**
When progress stalls, ask the team one question:

"What are we afraid might happen if we actually moved forward?"

Encourage open, honest answers — no judgment, no defensiveness. You'll often hear fears about losing control, failing publicly, or not being supported.
Once the fear is named, it loses its grip.

**Insight:**
Fear thrives in silence. When spoken aloud, it becomes wisdom.

Every fear reveals where trust needs to grow.

## 3. Energetic Reset Meetings

**Purpose:** To clear emotional buildup and restore team flow.

**How to do it:**

- Schedule a short 20-minute meeting at the end of any high-stress cycle or project.

- The agenda:

    1. What drained our energy this week?

    2. What gave us energy?

    3. What needs to be released before we move forward?

Let people share freely.
You're not solving problems — you're moving energy.

**Insight:**
This simple practice prevents emotional residue from hardening into resistance.

Energy clears through expression, not suppression.

## 4. The Flow Experiment

**Purpose:** To prove that trust creates faster results than control.

**How to do it:**
Pick one process that feels heavy — an approval step, a meeting cadence, a project protocol.
Simplify or remove it for 30 days.
Replace control with clarity: define the goal, then trust the team.

At the end of the trial, compare results.
Most companies find that efficiency, engagement, and morale rise — not because they worked harder, but because they worked lighter.

**Insight:**
Flow is not luck — it's what happens when energy stops being micromanaged.

Less resistance, more results.

## 5. The 24-Hour Observation Rule

**Purpose:** To transform reaction into reflection at the leadership level.

**How to do it:**
When something triggers frustration — a missed deadline, a disagreement, a dip in performance — resist the urge to react immediately.
Instead, observe for 24 hours.

Ask yourself:

- "What is this resistance showing me?"

- "Is this truly urgent, or emotionally charged?"

- "What might this situation be trying to teach us?"

In most cases, what felt like a problem reveals itself as a pattern — one ready to be healed.

**Insight:**
Observation is the first step in liberation.

Awareness dissolves resistance faster than action ever could.

**Energetic Takeaway**

Resistance is energy with a message.
When you stop seeing it as conflict and start treating it as communication, you convert friction into insight, and insight into flow.

Every time a company pauses to listen — truly listen — it moves closer to coherence.

Because the goal isn't to eliminate resistance; it's to evolve through it.

When you honor resistance, it becomes the force that carries you forward.

**Section 6: Reflection Prompts**

Resistance is never random — it's a messenger.
It appears to show us what we're ready to see, release, or realign.
Use these prompts as mirrors to interpret what your company's energy might be trying to say.

## For Leaders

**1. Where in the organization am I noticing repeated patterns of tension or stagnation?**
What do those patterns have in common — people, process, or mindset?
Patterns reveal what we've been unwilling to change.

**2. Do I tend to meet resistance with control, avoidance, or curiosity?**
What would happen if I chose curiosity every time?

**3. What am I afraid might happen if I truly let go of control?**
Would my identity as a leader shift?
Would I have to trust more deeply?

**4. When was the last time I admitted, "I don't know" — and allowed someone else to lead?**
Humility restores flow. The need to appear certain is one of leadership's biggest energetic blocks.

**5. Am I rewarding speed, or am I rewarding alignment?**
Fast decisions made from fear always cost more than slow decisions made from truth.

Great leaders don't eliminate resistance — they listen to it until it reveals the lesson.

## For Teams

**1. What part of our work feels consistently heavy or frustrating?**
If that task or process had a voice, what would it say?
Energy always expresses before people do.

**2. Do I feel safe to voice honest feedback or disagreement?**
If not, what would need to shift in our culture for me to feel that safety?

**3. What's one recurring issue we keep "working around" instead of addressing?**
Avoidance is unspoken resistance — and it accumulates like emotional clutter.

**4. Where do I personally feel resistance in my role?**
Is it resistance to change, to communication, to new leadership?
What might that resistance be trying to teach me about growth or boundaries?

**5. What part of our company's vision excites me — and what part scares me?**
Excitement and fear often point to the same door: expansion.

Every emotion is feedback. Every hesitation is direction.

**For the Organization as a Whole**

Use this in your next leadership retreat or culture meeting. Ask collectively:

"If our company were a living system — where would the energy feel stuck?"

Then pause.
Let the answers come without analysis.
You'll hear truths about communication, leadership, vision, or burnout — not as blame, but as opportunity.

Remember: resistance is always trying to move something forward. It's the company's higher self calling for alignment.

The moment you name the truth, energy starts to flow again.

**Energetic Reflection**

Every time you acknowledge resistance, you reclaim energy. Every time you listen without judgment, you dissolve the block. And every time you choose awareness over reaction, you invite transformation.

The presence of resistance doesn't mean something's wrong — it means something is awakening.

Resistance is not the wall. It's the whisper that says, "You're ready to grow."

**Section 7: Closing Affirmation**

There is a moment in every company's growth
when the push no longer works —
when more meetings, more effort, more control
only tighten what wants to expand.

That moment is not failure.
It's invitation.

Resistance is the company's soul saying,
"You're ready for something new."

When you stop fighting it, it softens.
When you stop judging it, it reveals.
When you listen to it, it teaches.

Resistance is not the wall — it's the doorway.

It's the pause before transformation.
The friction that sharpens focus.
The tension that invites truth.

Because evolution always creates pressure before it creates progress.
And alignment always asks us to let go of what can't come with us.

So breathe.
Don't rush to fix.
Feel what's heavy, name what's real, and release what's done.

As the energy clears, clarity will rush in.
The company will feel lighter.
The path will feel obvious.
And what once felt like resistance
will reveal itself as readiness.

Every block is just energy asking to move.
Every struggle is expansion in disguise.
Every pause is preparation for the next flow.

Let it move through.
Let it make you new.
And remember:
Resistance never comes to stop you —
it comes to show you how powerful you've become.

# Part Two — From Alignment to Expansion

# Chapter 8 — The Power of Language: How Words Shape Culture and Create Reality

**Living the Manifest Principles in Action**

You have journeyed through the **Seven Manifest Principles**, each one a foundation for creating an aligned and energetically coherent company.

You've explored:

- **Clarity**, where vision begins.

- **Belief**, where possibility anchors.

- **Emotional Alignment**, where energy harmonizes.

- **Inspired Action**, where movement ignites.

- **Detachment**, where trust replaces control.

- **Identity Alignment**, where truth becomes culture.

- **Overcoming Resistance**, where growth reveals itself.

These seven principles form the energetic architecture of business success — the inner system that determines everything from leadership presence to customer perception.
They are how a company comes into alignment with itself.

But alignment is not the end — it's the beginning.
Once energy flows freely, it seeks expansion.

Part Two is about that expansion.
It's where we move from understanding principles to living them — translating energy into language, leadership, trust, embodiment, and flow.
It's where alignment turns into influence, and where energy becomes impact.

This is the part where business stops being mechanical and becomes magnetic.

It's no longer about fixing systems; it's about **raising frequencies.**
No longer about what you do; it's about who you become.

The first half of this book taught you how to align.
The second half will show you how to expand —
how to lead, communicate, and create from energetic coherence.

Let's move forward —
from clarity to creation,
from intention to influence,
from alignment to expansion.

## Section 1: Words as Energy

"Language doesn't describe culture — it creates it."

Every organization has a sound.
Not the hum of computers or the ring of phones, but the energetic tone that lives inside its conversations.
You can feel it in the hallways, in the meetings, in the emails.
It's the vibration of the words people use — and those words shape everything.

Words are energy in motion.
They are frequencies that either expand or constrict the space they enter.
They build worlds inside a company — the invisible architecture of possibility or limitation.

When people say, "We're overwhelmed," the energy of that statement reinforces heaviness.
When they say, "We're in a growth phase," that same situation transforms into momentum.

Language is not neutral.
Every word carries a vibration, and that vibration becomes the emotional weather of the workplace.

What you speak about your company is what your company becomes.

## The Hidden Power of Everyday Language

Most companies underestimate the impact of their vocabulary.
They obsess over strategy and branding, yet overlook the daily phrases that shape culture.

- "We're putting out fires" creates an identity of chaos.
- "We're pivoting" creates an identity of adaptability.
- "We have to" carries pressure.
- "We get to" carries gratitude.

These subtle shifts in language create massive shifts in energy.
Because words don't just inform — they perform.
They don't describe what's happening — they decide what happens next.

Language is leadership in disguise.

## How Language Builds Culture

Culture is the accumulation of what's repeatedly said.
If meetings revolve around words like "problem," "issue," and "urgent," then the company vibrates at the frequency of survival.
But if the vocabulary shifts to "opportunity," "learning," and "evolution," then the same company vibrates at the frequency of creation.

Over time, this linguistic repetition becomes identity.
People stop thinking; they start speaking the company into existence.

That's why a company that says "we're different" but communicates in generic corporate language never truly feels different — because its energy still vibrates at sameness.

Every culture is the echo of its own language.

## Story: The Word Shift That Changed a Company

A marketing firm in Austin struggled with morale after a major reorganization. Teams were constantly saying things like "we're rebuilding," "we're behind," and "we need to catch up."

A new leader decided to change one word: instead of calling it a "rebuild," she called it a "rebirth."
That single linguistic shift reframed everything.

Suddenly, meetings opened with hope instead of exhaustion.
Projects felt like new beginnings, not recovery missions.
The same work, the same goals — but completely different energy.

Within months, employee engagement scores soared. Nothing mystical — just mindful language.

They didn't change the work. They changed the words — and the energy followed.

## Energetic Integrity in Communication

Every company has an energetic responsibility to the words it uses — internally and externally.
Because words either build trust or erode it.

If you say "people first" but your communication carries coldness or impatience, the energy reveals the truth.
If you say "innovation" but your tone says "fear," the vibration cancels the message.

Authenticity in language means that your words and your frequency match.
That's when communication becomes coherence — the alignment of thought, tone, and truth.

When words and energy align, communication becomes creation.

**Energetic Summary**

Language is the operating system of energy.
It tells the universe what you're ready to experience next.
And inside a company, it tells people what kind of energy they're allowed to express.

So choose your words with awareness.
Because they don't just tell your story — they set your vibration.

Language is energy made visible — what you speak, you shape.

**Section 2: The Science and Spirituality of Speech**

"Every word you speak is an instruction to your mind — and an invitation to the universe."

Language is the interface between thought and reality.
It's not just how we describe what we believe — it's how we build what we believe.
When you understand this, every conversation becomes a creative act.

Science calls it **neuroplasticity** — the brain's ability to rewire itself through repeated thought and language.

Spirituality calls it **vibration** — the energetic frequency that turns intention into manifestation.
They're the same truth, expressed in two languages:
one measured in neurons, the other in energy.

Both agree — words shape worlds.

## The Neuroscience of Speech

The human brain doesn't simply hear words — it feels them.
When you use words like safe, supported, inspired, the brain releases oxytocin, the chemical of trust.
When you use words like urgent, fail, crisis, it triggers cortisol, the hormone of stress.

So, a company's vocabulary literally determines its collective nervous system.
Repeated language of stress conditions the team into reactivity.
Repeated language of trust conditions the team into creativity.

Every "we're running out of time" plants a seed of scarcity.
Every "we're in perfect timing" plants a seed of faith.

The brain believes the words it hears most often.

That's why high-performing teams often have high-frequency language.
They talk in terms of what's possible, not what's missing.
Their language leads their energy — and their energy leads their results.

## The Energetics of Speech

From an energetic perspective, words are sound waves that carry intention.
They ripple through the field of a room, a company, a conversation — altering the emotional climate.

A single sentence can elevate an entire meeting or deflate it.
That's because energy responds instantly to tone, emotion, and authenticity.

When a leader says, "I believe in this team," and means it, everyone feels it.
That vibration travels faster than any memo or motivational email ever could.

But if the same words are spoken from fear or force, they land as static.
The vibration is off. The message doesn't penetrate.

It's never just what you say — it's the frequency you say it with.

## Where Science Meets Spirit

Science proves that language changes the brain.
Spirit teaches that language changes reality.
Together, they confirm that communication is both biology and magic
—
the most accessible form of manifestation we have.

When your company's language consistently reflects trust, creativity, and abundance,
you're not just "motivating" people — you're reprogramming their neural pathways to match success.

When your marketing copy or leadership message vibrates with genuine belief,
you're not just "branding" — you're broadcasting.

And when your culture shifts from fear-based words to empowered ones,
you're not just "retraining" behavior — you're recalibrating energy.

Language is the bridge between mindset and manifestation.

## Story: The Power of a Phrase

A luxury real estate firm used to describe slow months as being in a "sales slump."
Even though it was meant to be factual, the word slump carried defeat. After a workshop on energetic communication, the team replaced that phrase with "building momentum."

Every conversation that once began with pressure now began with possibility.
Agents spoke with more confidence, and clients felt the difference. The sales numbers followed — not because of new tactics, but new tone.

They had changed nothing but a phrase — yet changed everything about their frequency.

The word is the wand.

## Energetic Summary

The science of speech explains how language reshapes thought.
The spirituality of speech explains why it reshapes reality.

Together, they remind us that every word we speak — whether whispered in a meeting or written in a campaign — either expands energy or contracts it.

So speak deliberately.
Speak cleanly.
Speak with intention.

Because language is more than communication —
it's creation.

The brain rewires to your words. The universe responds to your vibration.

## Section 3: The Energetics of Internal Dialogue

"The words you speak about your company when no one's listening are the truest reflection of its vibration."

Every organization has two conversations:
the public one and the private one.

The public voice lives in press releases, marketing campaigns, and leadership emails.
The private voice lives in break rooms, internal chats, and unspoken thoughts.

Both carry energy — but it's the private one that shapes the company's true frequency.
Because that's the voice people feel.

If the internal dialogue is full of frustration, doubt, or gossip, no amount of polished branding can cover it.
But when the internal language hums with authenticity, care, and purpose, even simple communication radiates clarity and confidence.

Culture begins where conversations are most honest.

## The Inner Dialogue of an Organization

Internal dialogue isn't just what people say — it's what they believe while they say it.
When an employee says, "That's just how it is here," the energy behind that phrase carries resignation.
When someone says, "We're figuring this out," it carries movement.

You can hear an organization's health in its metaphors:

- Are people "putting out fires" or "building momentum"?

- Do they feel "burned out" or "ready to evolve"?

- Do they say, "We have to survive this quarter," or "We get to create what's next"?

Language reveals the state of belief.
And belief determines behavior.

Words are the mirrors of morale.

## How Negative Language Becomes Culture

When internal dialogue becomes habitually negative, it hardens into identity.
Phrases like "nothing ever changes here" or "leadership won't listen" start as feelings but end as energetic codes — instructions to the universe to keep proving them true.

This is how unconscious language turns into self-fulfilling prophecy.
The more often people repeat low-frequency words, the more energy the organization invests in that vibration.
And eventually, that vibration becomes the company's reality.

Internal language becomes external experience.

## Story: The Company That Rewrote Its Self-Talk

A hospitality brand realized that although they marketed warmth and joy, their internal meetings told a different story.
The team constantly used phrases like "we're drowning," "we can't keep up," and "this is just survival mode."

Leadership invited everyone to co-create a new internal vocabulary — phrases that matched their true intention.
"Drowning" became "learning to swim in deeper waters."

"Can't keep up" became "growing into our next level."
"Survival mode" became "building endurance."

The energy shifted instantly.
Meetings felt lighter.
Turnover dropped.
And guests began to comment on how the staff seemed "happier."

No new HR policy.
No rebrand.
Just new words — and therefore, new energy.

You don't change culture with programs. You change it with language.

## The Energy Behind "How We Talk About Us"

A powerful exercise for any company is to listen to the way people talk about "we."

When someone says "we," what emotion follows it — pride, weariness, excitement, apathy?
That's the company's energetic temperature.

A healthy "we" carries unity and purpose.
A resistant "we" carries fatigue or frustration.
And the difference isn't policy — it's frequency.

Language reveals whether a company believes in itself.

## Rewriting the Narrative

Changing internal dialogue begins with awareness:

- Notice recurring words or jokes that carry low energy.

- Replace habitual complaint phrases with neutral or empowering ones.
- Encourage team members to catch and reframe negative self-talk — "What's a better way to say this?"

This isn't about toxic positivity — it's about energetic precision. Because when words rise, energy rises with them.

Reframe the language, and you rewire the culture.

## Energetic Summary

Every company is talking to itself all the time — through meetings, Slack messages, side conversations, and leadership tone.
Those words either reinforce limitation or activate expansion.

If you want to change a company's vibration, start with its self-talk. Because words spoken in private become the energy experienced in public.

The story you tell about your company becomes the story the world believes.

## Section 4: Language of Leadership

"Leadership isn't what you say — it's the energy people feel when you speak."

Words from leaders carry a different weight.
They don't just communicate goals; they set the energetic tone of the entire organization.
A single sentence from leadership can open hearts or close them, inspire movement or create hesitation.

That's because leadership language doesn't just inform — it imprints.
It defines what energy is safe to express, what emotions are acceptable,
and what behaviors are rewarded.

The leader's words become the company's weather.

## Tone as Transmission

Every word carries tone, and tone is energy in motion.
A directive delivered with calm confidence creates clarity.
The same directive delivered with tension creates contraction.

Employees don't just hear the content of a message — they absorb its
vibration.
A rushed tone transmits anxiety.
A measured tone transmits trust.
A detached tone transmits disconnection.

The same sentence — "We'll get through this" — can sound like
command or comfort depending on the energy beneath it.

Your tone is the frequency people align to.

## The Energetic Hierarchy

Energy always travels downward.
If leadership speaks from fear, the team operates from protection.
If leadership speaks from faith, the team operates from possibility.

That's why alignment at the top matters more than strategy — because
tone trickles.

A leader who communicates vision from expansion gives permission
for everyone else to dream.

A leader who communicates from scarcity unconsciously tells everyone to shrink.

The words themselves might sound positive, but if the vibration is off, the message won't land.

You can't speak abundance while vibrating fear.

### Story: The Leader Who Learned to Speak in Energy

A design agency CEO was known for brilliance — and bluntness.
Her team respected her but feared her.
When she spoke, the room fell silent — not from inspiration, but from contraction.

During an offsite retreat, she realized her words, though accurate, carried stress.
Her feedback often began with "I need you to…" instead of "Let's explore how we can…"
The content wasn't wrong — the energy was.

She began practicing intentional language: slower, present, collaborative.
Her meetings transformed.
Her team started contributing ideas again — not because they suddenly knew more, but because they finally felt safe.

Within months, the company's creative output doubled.

She didn't change her message — she changed her frequency.

### Words that Empower vs. Words that Erode

| Disempowering Language | Empowering Language |
| --- | --- |
| "You have to meet this goal." | "We get to achieve this together." |

| Disempowering Language | Empowering Language |
|---|---|
| "This needs to be fixed." | "Let's explore how to make this better." |
| "That's not possible." | "What would need to be true for that to work?" |
| "Who's responsible for this mistake?" | "What can we learn from this?" |
| "We don't have time." | "Let's prioritize what matters most." |

Language either creates pressure or permission.
The leader decides which.

Control speaks from fear. Empowerment speaks from trust.

## The Energetics of Listening

The most powerful leaders don't just speak differently — they listen differently.
Listening is an energetic act.
It tells others, "Your voice has value."
And when people feel heard, they align naturally.

When leaders interrupt, defend, or rush conversations, the energy constricts.
When they listen fully — not to reply, but to receive — the organization relaxes into coherence.

Listening is leadership without words.

## Speaking as Calibration

Language can either correct or calibrate.
Correcting points out what's wrong.
Calibrating points toward what's possible.

For example:

- Correction says, "This isn't right."

- Calibration says, "Here's how we can align it."

Calibration creates safety and movement.
It reinforces that improvement is part of growth, not punishment.
That's how language becomes a coaching tool rather than a control mechanism.

Calibrated language moves energy forward without friction.

## Energetic Summary

Leadership language is the company's tuning fork.
When leaders speak with clarity, trust, and intention, the entire organization vibrates at that same frequency.

Every word spoken in authority becomes a template for how others think, feel, and behave.
When that language is grounded in empowerment and authenticity, culture doesn't have to be managed — it evolves naturally.

Speak not to control, but to calibrate.
Speak not to impress, but to align.
Speak not to be heard, but to raise the frequency of those who are listening.

## Section 5: Manifest This in Your Company — Exercises

Language mastery begins with awareness.

Before you can elevate the vibration of your company's words, you must first hear them.

These exercises help you observe, refine, and realign the energy that travels through your communication each day.

## 1. The Word Audit

**Purpose:** To identify low-frequency or misaligned words that subtly shape company culture.

**How to do it:**
Gather a small team from different departments and collect examples of commonly used language:
emails, meetings, marketing copy, Slack messages, leadership updates.

Create two columns:

- Column A: Words we often use

- Column B: How those words feel energetically (heavy, neutral, light)

Discuss:

- Which words drain energy?

- Which words uplift?

- Which ones no longer match who we're becoming?

Replace low-frequency words with higher-energy alternatives.

**Example:**
"Deadline" → "Delivery goal"
"Problem" → "Opportunity"
"Busy" → "In flow"

**Insight:**
Language evolves as the company evolves. Your vocabulary should reflect your vibration.

Your words are your company's frequency palette — choose the colors wisely.

## 2. The Reframe Practice

**Purpose:** To turn reactive, fear-based language into empowering, forward-moving dialogue.

**How to do it:**
At your next meeting, have someone write down phrases that sound heavy, pressured, or negative.
At the end, read them aloud and collectively reframe each one into lighter, more aligned language.

**Examples:**

- "We don't have enough time" → "We'll focus on what matters most."
- "This isn't working" → "We're learning what works better."
- "We can't afford that" → "Let's explore creative ways to make that possible."

**Insight:**
Every reframe lifts the company's energetic ceiling.
The more you practice reframing, the more naturally your language (and culture) flows toward possibility.

Reframing isn't spin — it's energetic realignment.

### 3. The One-Word Intention

**Purpose:** To align team energy before any meeting or project.

**How to do it:**
At the start of each meeting, invite everyone to share one word that represents how they want the next hour to feel.
Words like clarity, connection, creativity, flow, calm, or focus set an energetic tone.

This simple ritual creates collective intention — a shared vibration.

**Example:**
Before a strategy meeting, someone says clarity.
Before a sales kickoff, someone says momentum.
Before a difficult discussion, someone says grace.

When intention is named, energy aligns.

A single word can harmonize an entire room.

### 4. The Communication Detox

**Purpose:** To reveal how often fear-based words appear unconsciously.

**How to do it:**
For one week, challenge your team to avoid three words:
**"Problem," "Busy,"** and **"Can't."**

Whenever someone catches themselves using one, they pause and rephrase.
The point isn't perfection — it's awareness.

After the week, debrief as a team:

- What changed in tone, mood, or mindset?

- How did it affect collaboration or creativity?
  You'll notice that removing low-frequency words creates space for new, empowered language to emerge.

When you detox your words, you detox your energy.

## 5. The Story Rewrite

**Purpose:** To consciously shift the company's narrative from survival to expansion.

**How to do it:**
As a leadership team, finish this sentence together:

"Our company used to be ___, but now we're becoming ___."

Examples:

- "We used to be reactive, but now we're intentional."

- "We used to chase, but now we attract."

- "We used to compete, but now we collaborate."

Display this new story in your office or internal channels.
Let it serve as a verbal declaration of energetic evolution.

**Insight:**
When you rewrite the story, you rewrite the vibration.
And when you speak it consistently, you live it.

Language is how culture remembers who it's becoming.

## Energetic Takeaway

Language is the instrument that tunes the organization.
When every word carries intention, the company hums with coherence.

These exercises don't just refine communication — they raise collective frequency.
Because when language is clean, energy is clear.
And when energy is clear, success flows effortlessly.

Speak consciously. Speak clearly. Speak as if your words are building your future — because they are.

## Section 6: Reflection Prompts

Language is a mirror.
It reflects the consciousness of the person — and the culture — speaking it.
The purpose of these prompts is to help you listen more deeply to your words, tone, and energy until awareness itself begins to shift the vibration.

### For Leaders

**1. How does my tone set the emotional temperature of the room?**
Do my words make people feel safe or pressured?
Do I leave people lighter, or heavier, after I speak?

**2. Do I use language to control or to empower?**
Am I speaking to prove I'm right — or to invite collaboration and trust?

**3. What are the phrases I say most often?**
Are they aligned with the kind of energy I want my team to feel daily?

**4. When I speak about challenges, do I use language of possibility or limitation?**
Do I unknowingly reinforce scarcity, urgency, or fear?

**5. Do my words match my intention?**
If not, where might my energy and communication be out of sync?

Leadership language is energetic leadership — every word calibrates the field around you.

## For Teams

### 1. How do we talk about our work when leadership isn't in the room?
Do we use language that lifts our energy or lowers it?

### 2. What's our go-to phrase when things get stressful?
Does that phrase expand possibility ("We've got this") or reinforce struggle ("This is a nightmare")?

### 3. How often do we speak about what's working vs. what's wrong?
Balance reveals vibration.

### 4. Do we use humor to uplift or to hide frustration?
Playfulness is healing — sarcasm can be disguised resistance.

### 5. How would it feel to make every conversation an energetic upgrade?
What new language could help us embody that daily?

Teams that speak consciously create cohesion effortlessly.

## For the Organization as a Whole

### 1. What three words best describe the tone of our company right now?
Are those words what we want to amplify into the marketplace?

### 2. How do our internal words (meetings, memos) compare to our external words (marketing, brand voice)?
Is there harmony between what we say and what we sell?

**3. What words could we retire — not because they're wrong, but because we've outgrown them?**
Language evolution equals energetic evolution.

**4. How might we train ourselves to listen for tone, not just content?**
Every conversation carries a vibration. Awareness is transformation.

When a company listens to its own language, it begins to hear its soul.

### Energetic Reflection

The real question is never, "What are we saying?"
It's "What are we creating with what we're saying?"

Every word leaves an imprint — in minds, in meetings, in the energetic field of the business.
So speak gently.
Speak clearly.
Speak with the awareness that language is not just how we describe reality — it's how we design it.

The company that learns to speak consciously becomes the company that manifests effortlessly.

### Section 7: Closing Affirmation

There is power in your voice.
Not the loudness of it — the truth of it.

Every word you speak carries frequency.
Every sentence you craft sends a signal.
Every tone you choose either opens energy or closes it.

Language is the invisible architecture of everything your business will ever become.

It shapes how people feel, how they think, how they act — and how the universe responds.

When your words align with clarity and purpose, they stop being communication and start being creation.
They call in the people, opportunities, and outcomes that match your vibration.

Speak as if your words are designing the culture — because they are.

Speak words that build trust, not tension.
Speak ideas that invite curiosity, not control.
Speak from belief, not from fear.

Because the world doesn't need louder leaders — it needs clearer ones.
Those whose words carry warmth, wisdom, and resonance.

When you speak with intention, every meeting becomes a meditation.
Every conversation becomes a collaboration.
Every message becomes a manifestation.

Every word is a seed.
Speak what you wish to grow.

## The Universe is Listening. Speak Clearly

# Chapter 9 — Energy & Frequency: The Invisible Advantage of High-Vibration Companies

"Energy doesn't lie. Frequency is the new strategy."

Every company emits a frequency — an invisible signal made of emotion, intention, and belief.
You can feel it in their emails, their branding, their culture, their customer interactions.
Some companies feel magnetic. Others feel heavy.
The difference isn't marketing. It's energy.

### Section 1: The Field of Business Energy

"Everything is energy, and business is no exception."

Every company is a living energetic ecosystem — made up of people, thoughts, emotions, and language that combine to form a single vibration.

You can sense it immediately:

- The creative buzz of a startup aligned with purpose.
- The calm confidence of a trusted luxury brand.
- The dense exhaustion of an organization running on fear.

Energy precedes action.
Frequency precedes success.

Before a company scales, innovates, or rebrands, it must first align its vibration — because energy determines what it attracts.

This invisible field is the true foundation of performance.
Marketing, systems, and structures are just the visible expressions of the company's inner frequency.

If your energy is clear, your results will be too.

## Section 2: Understanding Frequency

Frequency is the measurable rate of vibration of energy.
In human terms, it's the feeling tone of your presence.
In organizational terms, it's the collective mood, tone, and belief
system that defines how the company moves through the world.

High-frequency companies feel light, alive, inspired, magnetic.
Low-frequency companies feel stagnant, fearful, or overly transactional.

The higher the frequency, the faster energy flows — ideas move
quicker, collaboration deepens, results compound.
The lower the frequency, the slower energy moves — communication
breaks down, friction increases, growth stalls.

Your company's frequency determines its future.

Frequency is not about positivity — it's about coherence.
A company vibrating at high frequency isn't avoiding hard truths; it's
facing them with clarity and alignment.

The goal isn't perfection — it's purity of energy.

## Section 3: The Science of Vibration Meets the Art of Culture

Everything in the universe vibrates — including you, your team, and
your company.
From a physics standpoint, energy is constantly in motion, and
frequencies attract like frequencies.
From a leadership standpoint, that means:

- Energetic calm attracts solutions.

- Energetic chaos attracts more problems.

- Energetic trust attracts opportunity.

- Energetic fear attracts resistance.

Culture, therefore, is just collective vibration.
It's the emotional and energetic resonance shared among the people inside your business.

Culture is what happens when energy agrees.

That's why changing culture begins not with policy, but with energy calibration — shifting the frequency of communication, intention, and belief until the company vibrates as one coherent field.

When teams align energetically, collaboration becomes effortless.
Ideas flow faster.
Customers feel the difference.

Energy alignment is the new productivity hack.

## Section 4: The Signs of High and Low Frequency

### High-Frequency Companies Feel Like:

- Calm but focused.

- Lighthearted yet disciplined.

- Driven by purpose, not panic.

- Open to new ideas.

- Emotionally safe for authenticity.

- Guided by gratitude rather than greed.

### Low-Frequency Companies Feel Like:

- Overwhelmed, reactive, urgent.

- Emotionally flat or fearful.

- Overly bureaucratic or defensive.

- Focused on problems instead of possibilities.

- Disconnected from purpose and joy.

These energies can't be faked.
Even if your marketing screams "innovative," if your culture whispers "exhausted," the vibration tells the truth.

Energy is the brand beneath the brand.

The moment you raise frequency — through clarity, kindness, and coherence — your company's entire energetic signature changes.

And when the frequency rises, everything accelerates:
revenue, retention, recognition, and resonance.

## Section 5: How to Raise Company Frequency

Raising frequency doesn't require big budgets — it requires big awareness.

Here are the simplest, most profound ways to elevate energy:

1. **Start with Intention.**
   Every meeting, project, and message begins with an energetic choice:
   "What do we want this to feel like?"
   Clarity of feeling sets clarity of frequency.

2. **Lead from Calm, Not Chaos.**
   Calm is the highest competitive advantage.
   It creates safety, and safety allows brilliance to surface.

3. **Clean Up Communication.**
   Replace heavy words with high-energy language (see Chapter

8).
Words either drain energy or generate it.

4. **Infuse Gratitude.**
   Gratitude raises collective vibration instantly — it tells the universe, "We are ready for more."

5. **Release Resistance.**
   Every unsolved problem is just energy waiting to move.
   Acknowledge it, breathe, and ask: "What's trying to flow here?"

6. **Protect the Energy Field.**
   Don't tolerate gossip, cynicism, or chronic complaint.
   They lower frequency faster than anything else.

Every choice is an energetic decision.

## Section 6: Story — The High-Frequency Turnaround

A technology company was growing rapidly but internally collapsing. Departments were territorial, leadership was exhausted, and communication had turned transactional.

Instead of another strategic overhaul, the CEO brought in an energetic coach who reframed everything:

"You don't have a productivity problem. You have a frequency problem."

They began simple practices — morning gratitude huddles, energy checks before meetings, and permission to pause when communication felt tense.

Within three months, stress levels dropped 40%.
Turnover slowed.
Clients commented that "the energy just feels different now."

No new product, no reorg, no external push — just a recalibration of vibration.

They didn't change what they did. They changed how they felt doing it.

## Section 7: Reflection Prompts

### For Leaders:

1. What emotion most defines our workplace right now — and is that the emotion we want to scale?
2. Do my words, actions, and presence lift the room's energy or lower it?
3. When things feel "off," do I push harder or pause to realign?

### For Teams:

1. Where do we feel flow? Where do we feel friction?
2. What practices raise our energy instantly — humor, gratitude, creativity?
3. What drains it — and how can we shift that pattern together?

### For the Organization:

1. If our company had a frequency you could hear, what would it sound like?
2. Does that sound match the vision we're trying to manifest?

Energy can't be managed — it can only be raised.

## Section 8: Closing Affirmation

There is an invisible hum beneath everything you do.
It's the frequency of your company —

the vibration created by every decision, every word, every emotion, every act of belief.

When that frequency is low, growth feels forced.
When it is high, success feels inevitable.

You don't attract what you want —
you attract what you are.

Raise your energy,
and your opportunities will find you faster.
Speak from clarity,
and your audience will feel you deeper.
Lead from trust,
and your team will rise higher.

Because energy doesn't lie — it amplifies.
It's the truth beneath strategy, the magnet beneath marketing, the pulse beneath performance.

Frequency is the new competitive advantage.

When your company vibrates at coherence —
with clarity, care, creativity, and calm —
you don't have to chase momentum.
You become it.

# Chapter 10 — Co-Creation with the Universe: Building in Partnership with Energy

"You are not doing business alone — you are in constant collaboration with the universe."

## Section 1: The Universal Partnership

"When you align with the energy that created worlds, you stop forcing outcomes — and start flowing with them."

Every successful creation — from a company to a product launch to a single inspired idea — begins with collaboration between the seen and the unseen.
The universe is not separate from business; it is business.

The same intelligence that grows forests, moves tides, and aligns stars also fuels your inspiration, guides your timing, and orchestrates opportunity.
When you learn to work with that intelligence, rather than against it, your company stops chasing results and starts magnetizing them.

Most businesses operate as if success is entirely self-generated — "we make it happen."
But the highest-frequency organizations know the deeper truth: **they are conduits, not controllers.**

You don't have to push the river when you realize you're part of the current.

## Section 2: The Law of Co-Creation

Co-creation is the art of conscious collaboration with universal energy.
It honors that there are two forces at work in every outcome:

1. **Human effort** — strategy, structure, and discipline.

2. **Divine orchestration** — timing, synchronicity, and unseen support.

When these two harmonize, flow replaces force.
Effort becomes expression.
Manifestation becomes method.

The Law of Co-Creation can be summarized simply:

Align first, act second, allow always.

Alignment means tuning your energy to the vibration of what you desire.
Action means moving from inspiration, not obligation.
Allowance means trusting that unseen energy is managing the details you can't yet see.

Companies that master this law innovate more effortlessly, attract ideal opportunities, and seem to "luck" into perfect timing — not because they're lucky, but because they're aligned.

Synchronicity is just strategy at a higher vibration.

## Section 3: Signs of Co-Creative Flow

How do you know when your company is truly co-creating with the universe?
The evidence is energetic — and unmistakable.

**You'll notice:**

- Ideas arrive quickly and clearly.

- People show up at exactly the right time.

- Small decisions feel guided by intuition.

- Stress diminishes because trust replaces control.

- Results exceed what strategy alone could produce.

There's a feeling of being carried rather than pushing.
Momentum becomes magnetic.

Co-creation feels like alignment meeting assistance.

This is not mystical — it's mechanical in the energetic sense.
When your vibration matches your vision, universal energy amplifies it.
Everything you need begins to find you.

That's why intuitive companies often outpace analytical ones — they're willing to trust inspiration before evidence.

## Section 4: The Science and Soul of Synchronicity

Modern quantum physics describes energy as interconnected — a unified field responding to frequency and observation.
When you set a clear intention, your consciousness organizes energy to align with it.
That's the science behind what spiritual traditions have always known: attention is creation.

Every decision, meeting, and conversation is an energetic broadcast to the universe saying, "This is what we're ready for."

When that broadcast carries coherence — clarity, belief, emotional alignment — it transmits cleanly.
When it carries fear or doubt, the signal is static.

The universe responds to vibration, not vocabulary.

That's why co-creation begins with inner calibration.
You must become the frequency of the outcome you want before it appears.

From that place, life organizes itself to meet you halfway — clients call, timing clicks, resources appear.
It feels like magic, but it's resonance.

## Section 5: Story — The Business That Trusted Timing

A global hospitality brand spent months forcing the launch of a new wellness division.
Budgets were approved, ads were designed, but something felt "off."
Delays piled up — vendors backed out, launch dates shifted.

Finally, the founder paused and asked,

"Are we trying to control this — or co-create it?"

They pulled back, quieted the noise, and reconnected with their core intention: to serve healing energy, not just sell experiences.

Within weeks, a new partner appeared — perfectly aligned, offering deeper wellness expertise and a better distribution model.
The launch unfolded organically, and the division became one of their most profitable ventures.

Delays aren't denials — they're divine recalibrations.

When you surrender control, you make room for synchronicity.
And when synchronicity takes the lead, outcomes exceed imagination.

## Section 6: Manifest This in Your Company — Practices of Co-Creation

## 1. The Alignment Pause

Before major decisions, pause and ask:

"Is this action inspired or forced?"
If it feels heavy, wait.
If it feels light and alive, proceed.
Energy knows before logic does.

## 2. The Intention Statement

Write clear energetic intentions for projects:
"We intend for this launch to flow with ease, attract aligned partners, and serve with joy."
Read it before meetings. Speak it aloud. Energy listens.

## 3. The 10-Minute Stillness

Dedicate ten minutes daily for quiet connection — no phones, no strategy.
Just listen. Often, your best business guidance arrives in that silence.

## 4. The Let-It-Go List

List everything you're currently trying to control.
Then, consciously release it to the universe with gratitude:

"I allow this to unfold perfectly, in perfect timing."
Watch how solutions emerge once energy is freed.

## 5. The Gratitude Loop

At day's end, acknowledge three moments of flow —
the email that arrived at the right time,
the idea that appeared mid-conversation,
the delay that turned out to be protection.
Gratitude amplifies cooperation with the unseen.

The more you notice support, the more support notices you.

## Section 7: Reflection Prompts

**For Leaders:**

1. Do I lead from effort or from energy?

2. Where am I forcing what's meant to flow?

3. What might happen if I trusted timing more than control?

**For Teams:**

1. What examples of synchronicity have we already experienced?

2. How do we invite guidance — through intuition, stillness, or reflection?

3. How would it feel to see every project as a co-creation with something greater?

**For the Organization:**

1. What's our energetic relationship with the universe — transactional or trusting?

2. How often do we pause to align before we act?

3. Could our company operate as both strategy and spirit in harmony?

The more you trust unseen support, the more tangible it becomes.

**Section 8: Closing Affirmation**

There is an intelligence moving through your business.
It speaks through timing, intuition, and the quiet voice that says, "Wait," or "Now."
It arranges introductions, synchronizes opportunities, and turns setbacks into strategy.

You are not doing this alone.
You never were.

When you release the illusion of control,
the universe rushes in to collaborate.
When you align your intention with service,
the universe amplifies your impact.

There is no competition in co-creation — only collaboration with
something infinite.

So breathe.
Trust your intuition.
Act when inspired.
Allow when delayed.

You are the strategy, and the universe is the system.
Together, you are unstoppable.

When you move in partnership with the unseen,
business becomes less about effort and more about elegance.
Less about managing, more about magnetizing.
Less about doing, more about becoming.

The universe is not testing you — it's teaming with you.
And the moment you remember that,
your work transforms from performance to purpose.

You are not manifesting alone — you are manifesting with everything.

# Chapter 11 — Trusting the Process: The Art of Divine Timing in Business

"What's meant for you will never miss you — but it might not meet your deadline."

## Section 1: The Frequency of Faith

"Trust is not waiting — it's alignment without evidence."

In business, trust is often measured by data.
In energy, trust is measured by vibration.

To trust the process means to hold energetic coherence even when outcomes are delayed.
It's the ability to stay in alignment long enough for the universe to rearrange itself around your intention.

Every goal, project, or partnership has an energetic gestation period. Just like seeds need seasons to grow, manifestations need alignment and timing to unfold.

The companies that thrive long-term understand this universal rhythm. They don't panic during pauses — they prepare.

When you trust the process, you release attachment to how and when things manifest, and instead focus on maintaining the vibration of belief.

Patience isn't passive — it's magnetic stability.

## Section 2: The Energetics of Timing

Everything has a natural order.
The universe doesn't rush; it calibrates.

Divine timing is the synchrony between your desire and your readiness.
When you're fully aligned — emotionally, energetically, and
strategically — the opportunity arrives as if by magic.

But if the energy isn't coherent yet — if fear, doubt, or disorganization
are clouding the signal — the universe delays delivery not as
punishment, but as protection.

Think of divine timing as energetic precision:

- When the frequency of your business matches the frequency of
  the outcome, manifestation locks in.

- When it doesn't, the process holds until you're aligned.

Delay is often just destiny in progress.

Every "not yet" is really "not aligned yet."
And the moment the energy aligns, what felt impossible becomes
inevitable.

## Section 3: Story — The Launch That Wasn't Ready

A conscious lifestyle brand spent nearly a year preparing to launch a
new product line.
Everything looked perfect — packaging, marketing, partnerships — yet
somehow, the timing kept slipping.

Every delay felt like failure.
Until one day, a supplier error forced a total redesign.

That redesign led to a more sustainable material, a better aesthetic, and eventually, an award-winning product line that became their signature offering.

Later, the founder said,

"The universe didn't delay us. It was developing us."

Had they forced the earlier launch, they would have achieved mediocrity instead of mastery.
That's the brilliance of divine timing: it's not slower — it's smarter.

When the universe holds you back, it's often holding space for something better.

## Section 4: How Fear Interrupts Flow

Trust and fear cannot coexist.

When businesses stop trusting the process, they begin to force outcomes.
They overwork, overanalyze, and overreact — lowering their vibration in the process.

Fear turns creative energy into control energy.
And control blocks flow.

Signs of mistrust include:

- Constantly checking metrics for reassurance.

- Micromanaging people or projects.

- Confusing movement with progress.

- Saying "we have to make this happen" instead of "we get to allow this to unfold."

These actions send an energetic message to the universe: "We don't believe."

Faith is silent confidence. Fear is noisy control.

The moment you return to trust, energy begins to move again.
Flow resumes.
Ideas reappear.
The next step reveals itself.

The process never stops working — only our faith does.

## Section 5: The Alignment of Waiting

Waiting is an energetic skill.
It's the space where alignment deepens.

To trust divine timing doesn't mean doing nothing — it means doing what's aligned while releasing what's anxious.

Use the waiting season to refine your vibration:

- Strengthen clarity.

- Revisit your "why."

- Clean up your language.

- Raise your company frequency.

- Expand gratitude for what's already working.

When energy is clean, time speeds up.
When energy is chaotic, time slows down.

The universe measures readiness by resonance, not the calendar.

The paradox of divine timing is this:
the moment you stop grasping for it, it arrives.

**Section 6: Manifest This in Your Company — Practices of Trust**

**1. The Alignment Audit**
Ask your team: "Where are we forcing instead of flowing?"
List areas where you're pushing timelines, overanalyzing, or doubting.
Pause those, realign your energy, and trust that the next right move will
present itself.

**2. The Surrender Statement**
Before major initiatives, affirm together:

"We release the need to control the timeline. We trust that everything
unfolds in perfect order, with perfect people, at the perfect pace."
Write it, print it, and post it. Let it become part of your company
mantra.

**3. The 24-Hour Rule**
When something goes wrong — a delay, rejection, or disappointment
— wait 24 hours before reacting.
This pause gives the universe time to reveal its hidden perfection.

**4. The Energetic Posture**
Notice your body during moments of stress.
Are your shoulders tense? Is your jaw tight?
That's energy resisting flow.
Exhale. Release. Realign.
Trust lives in relaxation.

**5. The Evidence Journal**
Keep a record of times when things worked out better because they
didn't go as planned.

Review it during difficult seasons.
It becomes proof that the process is always working for you.

Every pause is part of your preparation.

## Section 7: Reflection Prompts

### For Leaders:

1. How do I respond when plans don't go according to plan?
2. Do I model patience and trust — or pressure and panic?
3. How can I hold calm energy even when outcomes are uncertain?

### For Teams:

1. What project or goal in our company might be in its "gestation phase"?
2. How can we use this time to refine, align, and strengthen rather than rush?
3. What examples from our past prove that timing always works in our favor?

### For the Organization:

1. How might trusting divine timing change the way we lead, plan, and execute?
2. Where do we need to surrender control to gain clarity?
3. What would our company feel like if we believed everything was unfolding perfectly?

Trust is the highest frequency a business can hold.

## Section 8: Closing Affirmation

There is timing beyond your calendar —
an orchestration unfolding on your behalf,
matching your vibration,
arranging your opportunities,
aligning your readiness with your reward.

When you rush, you resist it.
When you relax, you receive it.

The universe is never late — only precise.
Every detour, delay, and closed door is a redirection toward alignment.

Trusting the process is the art of staying faithful when evidence is
invisible.
It's knowing that even in stillness, the energy is working.

So release your timelines.
Surrender your urgency.
Breathe into the unfolding.

The process is perfect, even when it isn't comfortable.

Every great company, every visionary leader, every aligned creation has
mastered this truth:
you don't need to know how it will happen —
you only need to know it will.

Stay steady.
Stay open.
Stay believing.

Because when faith holds the frequency,
the universe always delivers on time.

Trust isn't waiting — it's knowing.

# Chapter 12 — Embodiment: Leading from the Frequency of Fulfillment

"You don't attract what you want — you attract what you are."

## Section 1: The Power of Embodiment

"Energy doesn't respond to words. It responds to who you've become."

Embodiment is the bridge between knowledge and reality.
It's the moment when what you teach, believe, and envision begins to live through you.

In business, embodiment means that your energy — not your strategy — leads.
You no longer have to convince people of your vision. They can feel it in your presence.

A company can publish values on a website, but until those values are lived in tone, behavior, and energy, they are only words.
Embodiment makes them truth.

When belief becomes being, manifestation becomes motion.

This is the frequency of fulfillment — the vibration of alignment fully expressed.
It's not just doing the work; it's being the work.

## Section 2: From Concept to Consciousness

Many leaders understand alignment intellectually but struggle to live it energetically.
They can recite the principles — clarity, belief, detachment, trust — yet still operate in fear, pressure, or control.

That's because embodiment isn't about remembering; it's about repatterning.
It's not mental — it's magnetic.

Embodiment happens when your emotional energy and your actions are in complete coherence.
Your words, decisions, and presence all communicate the same vibration.

Embodiment is internal congruence made visible.

It's what happens when you stop talking about balance and start radiating it.
When you stop strategizing authenticity and start being it.

The shift is subtle but seismic:
You move from thinking about alignment to emanating it.

And that changes everything — because the universe mirrors embodiment faster than intention.

## Section 3: The Embodied Leader

An embodied leader doesn't lead by effort — they lead by energy.

They don't push people; they pull energy.
They don't motivate through fear; they magnetize through coherence.
They don't demand alignment; they are alignment.

You can feel it when they walk into a room.
They don't have to say much — their calm, clarity, and conviction set the tone.

They're not reactive to external chaos because they understand that energy flows from the inside out.
They know that stability creates success, not the other way around.

True leadership is energetic stewardship.

An embodied leader trusts that their frequency speaks louder than their title.
They lead less from hierarchy and more from harmony.
Their presence doesn't command attention — it creates safety.

This kind of leader becomes a tuning fork for the entire organization.
When they're grounded, everyone else rises.

Your energy is your influence.

## Section 4: Embodiment in Company Culture

A company embodies energy the same way a leader does — through consistent vibration.

When the energy of the company matches its message, authenticity radiates through everything:

- The way employees speak.
- The way customers feel.
- The way decisions are made.

This is why culture cannot be faked.
If you preach collaboration but operate in competition, the vibration tells the truth.
If you advertise joy but lead with burnout, the frequency collapses.

A company's energy is its true brand identity.

Embodied culture means that everyone becomes a living example of the mission.
Not through rules — through resonance.

Employees don't need to memorize values; they simply feel them.
Meetings carry the same warmth as marketing.
Client interactions reflect the same integrity as leadership.

This is energetic congruence at scale —
the outer experience perfectly mirroring the inner vibration.

When a company lives its values energetically, its results become
inevitable.

## Section 5: Story — The Leader Who Became the Message

A creative agency founder built her company on the principle of
"energy first."
She meditated before client calls, began meetings with intention-setting,
and created space for her team to pause rather than push.

At first, some employees thought it was "too spiritual" for business.
But within months, they noticed a pattern: projects flowed smoother,
clients were happier, and new opportunities seemed to appear
effortlessly.

When asked what changed, one designer said,

"She stopped talking about alignment — she became it."

That single shift rippled through the company.
Her presence calibrated the team more than any system or speech
could.

Embodiment is silent leadership.

People don't follow what you say; they follow who you are.
When you become the embodiment of trust, creativity, and abundance,
you don't have to lead with force — you lead through frequency.

## Section 6: Manifest This in Your Company — Practices of Embodiment

### 1. The Energy Mirror
Before making major decisions, pause and ask:

"Does this choice reflect the energy of who we say we are?"
If the answer is no, realign before proceeding.
Embodiment means your vibration and your vision always match.

### 2. The Presence Practice
Start meetings with 60 seconds of collective stillness.
Allow everyone to arrive energetically before speaking.
The most powerful leadership presence is calm, not constant.

### 3. The Alignment Anchor
Choose one word that defines your company's ideal frequency — peace, innovation, joy, flow.
Display it visually. Speak it daily.
Let every action be filtered through it.

### 4. The Energetic Reset
When tension arises, invite a short "energy reset."
Three deep breaths, eyes closed, hands on heart.
Remind everyone: we are not fixing energy; we are resetting to alignment.

### 5. The Integration Journal
Encourage each team member to write weekly reflections:

- Where did I feel most aligned this week?

- Where did I feel off?

- What energy do I want to embody next week?
  This turns embodiment into an ongoing practice, not a concept.

Embodiment is maintenance of vibration.

## Section 7: Reflection Prompts

### For Leaders:

1. What energy do I bring into every room — calm or chaos, trust or tension?
2. Do my daily habits match the frequency I expect from my team?
3. How can I embody my company's purpose more clearly in tone, posture, and presence?

### For Teams:

1. When our company is in alignment, how does it feel?
2. What energy do we collectively radiate to clients and partners?
3. How can we remind each other to return to coherence when stress appears?

### For the Organization:

1. If our company's vibration could be seen, would it match our message?
2. What habits, words, or patterns are out of energetic integrity?
3. How might we turn embodiment into a daily ritual rather than a yearly retreat?

Embodiment is culture made visible.

## Section 8: Closing Affirmation

You have learned the principles.
You have practiced the alignment.
Now, you become the vibration.

Embodiment is mastery —
the moment when your being speaks louder than your doing.

It's the calm that anchors chaos,
the trust that transcends uncertainty,
the frequency that fuels fulfillment.

When you are embodied, you no longer chase success —
you radiate it.
Clients feel it.
Teams reflect it.
The universe amplifies it.

You don't manifest what you want.
You manifest what you've become.

So stand in your power.
Speak with coherence.
Lead with love.
Be the energy you wish your company to carry.

Because the future doesn't belong to those who work the hardest —
it belongs to those who vibrate the highest.

When you embody alignment,
you don't have to reach for abundance.
Abundance reaches for you.

The most powerful business strategy is embodiment

# Chapter 13 — Receiving Mode: Opening the Flow of Abundance in Business

"What you desire is already here. The question is — are you open to receive it?"

## Section 1: The Energy of Allowing

"You don't attract abundance — you allow it."

The universe is constantly offering opportunities, ideas, clients, partnerships, and possibilities.
But most companies and leaders are too energetically closed to receive them.

Receiving Mode is not about passivity; it's about permission.
It's the willingness to be open — emotionally, energetically, and strategically — to what's ready to flow in.

Most organizations are overtrained in effort and undertrained in allowance.
They believe results must be earned through exhaustion instead of aligned through energy.
But abundance doesn't respond to effort — it responds to openness.

Effort creates movement. Openness creates momentum.

When a business finally relaxes into trust, its vibration lifts.
And in that higher frequency, everything that's been trying to reach it — clients, ideas, opportunities — finally can.

## Section 2: The Law of Reception

The universe is reciprocal — it mirrors the energy you hold.
If your frequency says "I already have enough," it multiplies that.
If it says "I'm desperate for more," it mirrors scarcity.

Receiving Mode is the energetic balance between giving and allowing.
Too much giving creates depletion.
Too much controlling creates blockage.

To receive fully, a company must first believe it deserves to.
That belief opens the energetic field.

The Law of Reception operates like a magnetic current:

- You give with clarity.

- You allow with gratitude.

- You receive with humility.

When this flow is open, your business becomes a channel rather than a container — energy moves through it freely and abundantly.

Receiving is not taking — it's allowing energy to circulate through you.

## Section 3: The Blocks to Receiving

Every company and leader has energetic blocks that prevent abundance from arriving.
These blocks are usually invisible — emotional, cultural, or habitual patterns that constrict flow.

**The most common blocks include:**

1. **Overcontrol:** The belief that everything must be forced or micromanaged.

- ○ Energy Message: "I don't trust flow."

2. **Unworthiness:** A hidden sense of not deserving success or ease.

   - ○ Energy Message: "Abundance belongs to others, not me."

3. **Busyness Addiction:** Constant motion to prove value.

   - ○ Energy Message: "I must do more to deserve more."

4. **Fear of Visibility:** The resistance to being fully seen or celebrated.

   - ○ Energy Message: "I'm not safe being recognized."

5. **Scarcity Mindset:** The subconscious belief that there's not enough — time, money, clients, or opportunity.

   - ○ Energy Message: "I can't receive because others will lose."

Each of these beliefs creates energetic contraction —
and contraction repels abundance.

You can't receive from a clenched fist.

When a company releases these blocks — through awareness, self-trust, and gratitude — it opens the channel for abundance to move again.

## Section 4: Story — The Business That Learned to Receive

A marketing firm known for brilliant creative work had plateaued. Despite incredible results, revenue remained stagnant.

The founder realized she was always giving — to clients, to employees, to projects — but rarely allowing herself or her business to receive. She would discount fees, overdeliver, and avoid asking for referrals.

She began a simple practice: before every new project, she declared,

"We are open to receive all forms of abundance — financial, creative, and relational."

Within six months, the company's largest client doubled their budget, new referrals flowed in, and she received an unexpected media feature highlighting her firm's unique energy-based approach to branding.

When she stopped trying to earn abundance and started allowing it, everything expanded.

The universe can't deliver what you won't accept.

## Section 5: The Energetics of Gratitude

Gratitude is the frequency that unlocks receiving.
It tells the universe, "I already have enough, and I'm ready for more."

Gratitude shifts your attention from lack to abundance, immediately aligning your vibration with expansion.
That's why it's one of the most powerful business tools you can practice.

High-frequency companies don't just thank customers — they thank energy.
They express appreciation for timing, flow, and even challenges.

Because they know that gratitude transforms resistance into readiness.

Gratitude is the language of receivership.

Daily gratitude rituals — team acknowledgments, written reflections, or even "thank you" pauses at the end of meetings — amplify abundance exponentially.

The more you recognize what's already flowing, the faster more arrives.

Every thank you is an energetic 'yes' to more.

## Section 6: Manifest This in Your Company — Practices of Receiving

### 1. The Open-Channel Check-In
At the start of each week, ask:

"Where are we open to receive? Where are we blocking flow?"
Encourage honesty — even small fears, doubts, or control patterns can constrict abundance.

### 2. The Balanced Exchange
Ensure energy flows both ways — value for value.
Charge fair prices. Receive fair recognition.
Refuse to discount your worth.

Undercharging is an energetic leak.

### 3. The Gratitude Roundtable
End every team meeting with one thing each person appreciates — about a colleague, a client, or the process itself.
Gratitude expands collective vibration faster than any motivational talk.

### 4. The Receiving Ritual
After each success — a new client, a great review, a milestone — pause and say aloud:

"We receive this with joy, gratitude, and expansion."
Receiving consciously turns events into energetic anchors.

### 5. The Abundance Audit
Review your systems, pricing, and boundaries.

Ask: "Does this structure allow for flow, or does it create friction?" Make practical and energetic adjustments accordingly.

When you open space, abundance fills it.

## Section 7: Reflection Prompts

### For Leaders:

1. Where in my leadership am I still forcing instead of allowing?
2. How comfortable am I with ease, praise, or prosperity?
3. Do I believe that receiving is as sacred as giving?

### For Teams:

1. Are we operating from gratitude or from pressure?
2. How do we celebrate success — with joy or with guilt?
3. Where might we unconsciously block abundance (through overwork, doubt, or self-criticism)?

### For the Organization:

1. What is our energetic relationship with abundance — open, neutral, or resistant?
2. Do our policies and pricing reflect self-worth?
3. How would our company look and feel if we allowed abundance without guilt?

You expand what you feel worthy of receiving.

## Section 8: Closing Affirmation

Abundance is not earned — it's allowed.
It doesn't come from striving harder, but from surrendering deeper.

You've already done the work.
You've already aligned your energy.
Now, the only task left is to receive.

Let go of guilt.
Let go of force.
Let go of the old identity that believed success had to be chased.

You are no longer the seeker. You are the receiver.

As you open your energy to receive, the universe rushes in to fill the space.
Clients appear. Partnerships align. Ideas flow.
The outer world finally mirrors the inner readiness you've built.

So take a breath.
Relax your grip.
Smile at what's arriving.

You've already manifested it — now you're just watching it unfold.

The greatest business skill is the ability to receive with grace.

Because when you open to abundance,
you don't just grow your company —
you expand the universe itself.

# Chapter 14 — Integration: The Embodied Organization

"Integration is where knowledge becomes culture and energy becomes identity."

## Section 1: The Whole Company as One Field

"Integration is not the end of transformation — it's the embodiment of it."

Integration is where alignment becomes automatic.
It's when the principles you've learned stop living in your notes and start living in your decisions, your communication, your culture, and your energy.

When a company integrates the Manifest Principles, it no longer needs to "apply" them — it is them.
They become the invisible rhythm behind every meeting, message, and moment.

Integration is not about adding more; it's about becoming whole.
Every principle — Clarity, Belief, Emotional Alignment, Inspired Action, Detachment, Identity Alignment, Overcoming Resistance, and the rest — harmonizes into one coherent frequency.

An integrated organization doesn't chase success — it channels it.

## Section 2: From Practice to Presence

Every transformation begins with learning, deepens through practice, and completes through presence.
Presence means you no longer have to remember the principles because you naturally embody them.

Clarity lives in your communication.
Belief pulses through your confidence.
Emotional alignment shapes your tone.
Inspired action fuels your motion.
Detachment anchors your peace.
Trust becomes your default.
Embodiment defines your leadership.
Receiving amplifies your results.

This is what happens when your internal energy and external reality
merge —
your company becomes consciousness in motion.

Presence is integration in its purest form.

When a team reaches this stage, strategy feels effortless, culture feels
alive, and results feel natural.
It's not magic — it's mastery.

## Section 3: The Energetics of Wholeness

Integration is the vibration of wholeness.
It's when there are no longer competing energies within the
organization — no separation between intention and action, between
message and energy, between leadership and culture.

In a fragmented company, departments compete, values conflict, and
goals collide.
In an integrated one, every part moves with the same heartbeat.

That's what coherence feels like —
a unified field of energy where everyone is operating from alignment
rather than ego.

Wholeness is not perfection — it's unity of vibration.

When energy flows freely through the organization, creativity rises, innovation accelerates, and collaboration feels easy.
Integration replaces hustle with harmony.

You stop trying to manage people and start orchestrating energy.

## Section 4: Story — The Organization That Became Its Message

A luxury homebuilder once hired a branding agency to "make us look more intentional."
The agency realized that the company didn't have a brand problem — it had an energy problem.
Externally, they spoke about craftsmanship, care, and connection.
Internally, they operated from pressure, perfectionism, and burnout.

Through a year of energetic coaching, leadership alignment sessions, and language recalibration, the company shifted its vibration.
They slowed meetings down, celebrated small wins, and began using language that reflected trust instead of tension.

Within eighteen months, their sales grew 40% — without new marketing.
What changed was not the message, but the energy behind the message.

They didn't rebrand their company — they re-calibrated their consciousness.

The result: customers began saying, "You can feel the difference."

That's the power of integration — when who you are and what you say finally vibrate at the same frequency.

## Section 5: The Practices of Integration

Integration is a continual process — a rhythm of remembering and realigning.
Here are ways to keep your organization in integrated flow:

## 1. The Energy Review

Once a quarter, gather your team and reflect:

- Where did we act from alignment?

- Where did we react from fear?

- What energy do we want to carry forward?

Celebrate coherence as much as performance.

## 2. The Daily Alignment Minute

Begin every day or meeting with one minute of silence, breath, or intention.
Ask, "What's the energy we choose to bring today?"
That single minute anchors the entire company's vibration.

## 3. The Principle Reflection

Choose one Manifest Principle per month and integrate it consciously into operations.
For example:

- Month 1: Emotional Alignment in leadership conversations.

- Month 2: Detachment in sales goals.

- Month 3: Receiving Mode in client feedback.

This keeps energy alive through rhythm, not routine.

## 4. The Integration Check

Before major initiatives, ask:

"Does this decision align with who we've become?"
If it doesn't, pause and adjust.

## 5. The Embodiment Circle

Create monthly gatherings for open dialogue — no agenda, just energy.
Ask each person:

- Where did you feel most in flow?
- What lesson from the Principles helped you lead differently this month?
  Integration happens through sharing — vibration multiplies when witnessed.

Integration is sustained through ritual.

## Section 6: Reflection Prompts

### For Leaders:

1. Do I lead from alignment or urgency?
2. How consistent is my energy with the message I share?
3. Where can I integrate the Principles more deeply into my daily behavior?

### For Teams:

1. Do our words and actions feel like they come from the same energy?
2. How can we keep our work environment energetically clear and inspired?

3. Which Manifest Principle most transformed how we collaborate?

**For the Organization:**

1. If an outsider observed our company, could they feel our alignment?
2. How can we ensure that growth never outpaces our vibration?
3. What systems or rituals help us stay in integrity with our energy?

Integration is the ongoing dialogue between energy and action.

## Section 7: The Evolution of Conscious Business

The companies that will define the future are those that operate from energetic intelligence.
They will no longer separate intuition from strategy or profit from purpose.
They will understand that alignment creates efficiency, coherence creates innovation, and energy creates expansion.

This is the era of conscious business —
organizations that treat energy as currency, clarity as culture, and trust as infrastructure.

Integration is the final phase of evolution —
where spirituality and strategy merge into one seamless flow.

The new ROI is Resonance of Intention.

When a business vibrates at coherence, it not only succeeds — it serves.
Its energy uplifts employees, customers, communities, and even the industry around it.

That's the ripple effect of integration:
when one company becomes whole, it quietly heals the collective.

**Section 8: Closing Affirmation**

You've journeyed through all the principles —
from clarity to embodiment, from energy to trust, from receiving to
wholeness.

You've built a framework not just for business success,
but for conscious leadership, vibrant culture, and energetic evolution.

Integration is not a final destination —
it's a way of being.

It's the moment when every meeting becomes mindfulness,
every conversation becomes co-creation,
every result becomes reflection.

Your company is now a living field of alignment.

Operate from peace.
Decide from clarity.
Communicate from coherence.
Lead from love.

When energy, intention, and action move as one,
you no longer need to manifest — you simply magnetize.

So step fully into integration.
Be the embodied organization.
Be the proof that business can be both purposeful and prosperous,
both visionary and vibrational.

Because when you lead from wholeness,
you don't just build a company —
you build a consciousness.

# Chapter 15 Energy Before Strategy*

There is a moment that every leader, every salesperson, every founder eventually faces: the moment where the plan is perfect on paper... and yet something still feels off.

The strategy is sound.
The steps are clear.
The team is capable.
The goals are measurable.

And yet the results stall.

This is the moment where you learn one of the most powerful truths in business:

**Energy comes before strategy.**
**Every. Single. Time.**

Because business is not only a collection of processes, meetings, budgets, and data points. Business is a living, breathing ecosystem of human beings—each with beliefs, emotions, perceptions, fears, and motivations. The energy behind the work affects the outcome of the work.

You can have the best strategy in the world, but if the energy is off—yours or the team's—the outcomes will reflect that misalignment. Likewise, you can have an imperfect strategy paired with aligned, clear, committed energy—and the results will often exceed expectations.

Energy is the invisible variable driving business outcomes.
It is the unspoken difference between teams that feel unstoppable and teams that feel stuck.
It is the reason certain leaders inspire while others simply manage.
It is the reason some brands feel magnetic and others feel forgettable.

In this chapter, we explore how to intentionally **lead, sell, create, and operate from aligned energy**, and how this single shift elevates productivity, culture, engagement, customer experience, and the bottom line.

## The Energic Signature of a Leader

Every leader carries an energetic signature into the room.

Before you speak, before you present, before you negotiate, before any slides are shown… people feel you.

Your team reads your energy more than your words.
Your clients respond to your tone more than your pitch.
Your colleagues sense your confidence before they hear your reasoning.

This is why a calm leader can de-escalate chaos in seconds.
This is why a panicked leader can send shockwaves of fear through an entire department.
This is why a visionary leader can inspire teams to attempt the impossible.

People align themselves to the energy they are led by.

Your presence sets the temperature of the room.

When you walk in distracted, frustrated, rushed, or depleted, the energy of the meeting shifts. Projects stall. Conversations get heavier. Creativity decreases. People become more guarded.

But when you walk in grounded, clear, prepared, centered, and open, the entire room rises to meet you there. Ideas flow more freely. People become more receptive. Difficult conversations become productive. Decision-making becomes easier.

This is not "soft leadership."
This is the foundation of effective leadership.

Your energy is contagious—positively or negatively.

The question becomes:

**What energy am I leading with right now, and what energy do I expect others to mirror?**

You cannot expect trust if you lead with doubt.
You cannot expect enthusiasm if you lead with exhaustion.
You cannot expect creativity if you lead with constriction.
You cannot expect alignment if you lead from misalignment.

Your team does not follow your strategy.
They follow your energy through your strategy.

**When Energy Doesn't Match the Outcome**

Every business outcome is preceded by an energetic state.

Here's what that looks like in real life:

- A sales team that feels pressure and scarcity starts getting more no's—even with the same script.
- A marketing team that feels overwhelmed delivers generic campaigns—even with strong data.
- A CEO who feels disconnected from the company vision unintentionally signals instability—even without saying a word.
- A customer success team that feels underappreciated becomes reactive rather than proactive—even with clear KPIs.

Energy misalignment shows up in behavior long before it shows up on the balance sheet.

When outcomes aren't matching effort, the first question shouldn't be "What's wrong with the strategy?"
but rather
**"What's happening with the energy behind the strategy?"**

This is where the greatest leaders excel:
They don't only manage performance—they manage energy.

## The Meeting Before the Meeting

One of the simplest and most effective tools for leaders is what I call *The Meeting Before the Meeting*.

It's a short, intentional pause to align your energy before you walk into any important interaction.

It can take 30 seconds or 3 minutes.

The purpose is simple:
**You choose the energy you are bringing into the room instead of letting the day choose it for you.**

Here's how you do it:

1. **Stop.**
   Before opening the door, clicking "Join," or walking into the office.
2. **Breathe.**
   One slow deep breath to reset your nervous system.
3. **Ask:**
   *"What energy would make this meeting successful?"*
4. **Choose one word:**
   – Clear
   – Open
   – Decisive
   – Confident
   – Curious
   – Grounded
   – Optimistic
5. **Step into the meeting embodying that word.**

The difference is immediate and measurable.

A leader who walks in intentional creates an environment where alignment becomes possible.

A leader who walks in reactive creates an environment where tension becomes inevitable.

## When Your Energy is Out of Alignment

Even the best leaders get disconnected sometimes. The key is recognizing it quickly.

Here are common signs that your energy is off:

- You're forcing outcomes.
- You're overthinking small decisions.
- Every task feels heavier than it should.
- You're operating from urgency instead of clarity.
- You're reactive instead of responsive.
- You're worrying about what could go wrong.
- You're micromanaging because you don't trust the process.
- You feel disconnected from the bigger vision.

This isn't a strategy problem.
This is an energetic one.

When energy is out of alignment, strategy becomes harder than it needs to be.

The solution is not to work harder.
The solution is to realign your internal state.

Because here is the truth:

**The energy you create from determines the outcome you create.**

## The Cost of Misaligned Energy in Business

Misaligned energy has a real cost—financially, culturally, and operationally.

## 1. Productivity Drops

Teams mirror the emotional tone of leadership.
When the energy is scattered, productivity becomes inconsistent.

## 2. Creativity Shrinks

Creativity requires openness, safety, and confidence.
Misaligned energy creates tension, which suppresses innovation.

## 3. Decision-Making Slows Down

Fear-based energy creates over-analysis.
Aligned energy creates clarity and conviction.

## 4. Team Morale Declines

People feel the difference between a leader who is present and one
who is checked out.

## 5. Customer Experience Suffers

Clients feel misalignment instantly.
They feel rushed calls, tight energy, and low enthusiasm long before
they consciously recognize it.

## 6. Burnout Increases

When energy doesn't match the workload, emotional exhaustion
builds.

This is why some quarters feel smooth and abundant while others feel
heavy and strained—even under similar conditions.

Energy determines momentum.

## The Science Behind Energetic Leadership

This is not theoretical. It's measurable.

When leaders operate from aligned energy:

- **Cortisol drops**
  (People feel safer around you, increasing trust and communication.)
- **Prefrontal cortex activation increases**
  (The brain's creative, strategic center opens up.)
- **Mirror neurons fire**
  (Teams unconsciously synchronize with a leader's tone, posture, and pace.)
- **Emotional contagion**
  (Positive or negative energy spreads through an organization within minutes.)

When people say,
"I don't know why, but today everything feels better,"
what they're usually feeling is a shift in leadership energy.

## The Energetic Sales Leader

Sales is the clearest example of energy before strategy.

Two salespeople with the same pitch can get completely different results based solely on energy.

Clients feel:

- confidence vs desperation
- certainty vs doubt
- enthusiasm vs routine
- presence vs distraction
- abundance vs scarcity

Sales doesn't start with a script.
It starts with state.

Your energy communicates before your words do.

When you approach a client believing:

*"This is a win for both of us."*

Everything shifts.

Your tone becomes warmer.
Your pacing becomes calmer.
Your confidence becomes grounded.
Your listening becomes deeper.
Your intuition sharpens.
Your presence strengthens.

Clients may never articulate it, but they feel it instantly.

## The Energetic CEO

The most successful CEOs are masters of energetic leadership. They know:

- When to elevate the room.
- When to create calm.
- When to bring vision.
- When to create urgency.
- When to create safety.
- When to create space.

Their presence is intentional.
Their decisions are grounded.
Their communication is clean.
Their energy is stable—even when the business isn't.

Employees don't need their CEO to be perfect.
They need them to be clear, consistent, and energetically aligned.

When the CEO is steady, the company becomes steady.

## The Energetic Entrepreneur

Entrepreneurs often make the mistake of thinking:

"I just need the perfect plan."
"I need the right mentor."

"I need more time."
"I need to fix this one thing first."

But entrepreneurship is 90% energetic leadership and 10% strategy.

The projects that grow the fastest are the ones infused with the most aligned energy—not the ones with the longest business plans.

If you want to attract:

- collaborators
- investors
- customers
- opportunities
- visibility
- strategic partnerships

...it won't come from effort alone.

It comes from alignment.

People are drawn to entrepreneurs who radiate confidence, clarity, purpose, and momentum.

## Real Life Example of a Sales Call That Changed Everything

A sales director once shared how she walked into a high-stakes meeting after a morning of chaos. Traffic delays. Email overwhelm. A missed call from her CEO. Her energy was scattered and tense.

She delivered the pitch flawlessly—but the client declined.

A week later, she met the same client again.
This time, she took 60 seconds before the meeting to align her energy. She chose the word *presence*. She walked in calm, open, and grounded.

The conversation changed.
The client was more relaxed.

The dialogue felt natural.
The pitch became a conversation, not a presentation.

They said yes.

Same product.
Same pricing.
Same strategy.
No new slides.
No new objection handling.

Only one thing changed: **her energy.**

## The Most Underrated Sales Skill – Self Regulation

Emotional regulation is no longer a "soft skill."
It's a performance skill.

The leaders who excel are not the ones who avoid stress—they're the ones who can **return to alignment quickly**.

Here are the most effective ways:

### 1. The 10-Second Reset

A slow exhale signals safety to your brain.
This alone drops your stress response.

### 2. The State Question

Ask: *"What energy is required of me right now?"*
This shifts you out of reactivity into leadership.

### 3. Micro-Grounding

Place both feet on the floor.
Feel your body in the chair.
Instant regulation.

## 4. Energetic Reframing

Shift from:
*"This is urgent."*
to
*"This is solvable."*

## 5. The Posture Reset

Lift your chest slightly.
Open the shoulders.
The body signals to the mind: "We're in control."

These techniques take seconds, yet they change meetings, interactions, and outcomes.

### The Energetic Culture of a Team

Teams take on the energy of:

- their leader,
- the environment,
- the expectations, and
- the emotional norms of the group.

High-performing teams have:

- high trust
- high clarity
- high communication
- high accountability
- low drama
- low fear
- low confusion
- low resistance

This is not accidental.
It is cultivated through intentional leadership.

When a leader manages energy, the team becomes more resilient, more autonomous, more collaborative, and more innovative.

## How to Set an Energetic Standard in Your Company

### 1. Start Meetings with State, Not Status

Instead of:
"Any updates?"
Try:
"What's one win, one focus, and one energy we're bringing today?"

### 2. Normalize Grounding Before Big Decisions

A 30-second pause leads to better outcomes than rushing.

### 3. Model the Behavior

If you want calm—be calm.
If you want creativity—be open.
If you want accountability—be accountable.

### 4. Communicate with energetic intention

Not just what you say—but how you say it.

### 5. Protect your team's emotional bandwidth

Not every fire deserves their energy.

As a leader, you are the energetic gatekeeper.

### When Strategy Finally Meets Energy

The magic happens when:

- your strategy is aligned
- your execution is consistent

- your decisions are clean
- your communication is grounded
- your presence is intentional
- your vision is compelling
- your energy is congruent with your outcomes

This is when a business becomes unstoppable.

Projects move faster.
Teams take ownership.
Opportunities appear.
Clients become advocates.
Revenue grows more naturally.

Because the energy behind the work matches the result you want.

**Your Leadership Energy Practice**

Use this as a daily or weekly guide:

## 1. Choose your leadership energy for the week

One word: calm, decisive, grounded, visionary, open, confident.

## 2. Align your actions with that energy

Is this decision coming from fear or clarity?
Is this email coming from pressure or presence?

## 3. Audit your energy daily

What drained me?
What fueled me?
Where was I reactive?
Where was I aligned?

## 4. Realign quickly when off-track

Pause → Breathe → Choose again.

## 5. Protect your energetic boundaries

Not every problem deserves access to you.
Not every meeting deserves your full bandwidth.
Not every demand is urgent.

### The Final Truth About Energy in Business

The world teaches leaders to prioritize:

- strategy
- KPIs
- analytics
- logistics
- processes
- goals

These matter—deeply.

But none of them work optimally without aligned energy behind them.

Because the most successful leaders, teams, and companies in the world share one truth:

**Energy is the foundation.**
**Strategy is the structure.**
**Results are the natural outcome.**

When you align the energy, the strategy becomes easier.
When you align the energy, the team becomes cohesive.
When you align the energy, the work becomes lighter.
When you align the energy, the outcomes become inevitable.

You lead differently.
You sell differently.
You communicate differently.
You create differently.
You operate differently.
You inspire differently.
You *become* a different leader.

And that is when everything in business begins to shift in your favor.

# Notes & Manifestations in Business:

# Ideas to Implement:

# My Vision in Motion:

**Execution Notes:**

# Creative Planning Space:

# Growth Strategies:

# Epilogue — The Light You Lead With

"You are not just building a business — you are building energy that will outlast you."

If you've made it here, you've already shifted.
You've read the words, but more importantly, you've felt them.
Something inside you has expanded — not because you learned something new,
but because you remembered who you are.

You've always known that leadership was more than strategy,
that culture was more than meetings and metrics,
that success was never about effort alone —
it was always about energy.

This book wasn't meant to teach you how to work harder,
but how to **work higher.**
To lead from coherence.
To speak from clarity.
To act from trust.

Because business — when done with consciousness — becomes a spiritual practice.
It becomes the place where your growth and your impact meet.

## You Are the Manifest Principle

You don't need another framework.
You are the framework.

Every principle you've read —
Clarity, Belief, Emotional Alignment, Inspired Action, Detachment,

Identity Alignment & Overcoming Resistance,
already lives within you.

They aren't separate steps to master; they're frequencies you return to.
Moments of remembering.
Breaths of alignment.

You'll notice them when you pause before reacting.
When you choose to trust instead of push.
When you see challenge as calibration instead of chaos.

You are not applying the principles — you are living them.

## The Company You Keep — and Keep Becoming

Your business is a mirror of your energy.
It grows when you grow.
It expands when you soften.
It succeeds when you surrender control and let flow lead.

Let your company be an expression of your evolution.
Let it breathe, flow, and change shape as you do.

You don't have to get everything perfect.
You just have to stay in tune.

When you move in clarity and trust,
the right people find you.
The right opportunities align.
The right timing unfolds.

You are not managing a business — you are tending a vibration.

## The Closing Breath

Take one deep breath.
Inhale clarity.
Exhale resistance.

Remember — you are always co-creating with the universe.
Every meeting, every idea, every decision is a dialogue between your
energy and the infinite.

So keep your vibration clear.
Keep your faith steady.
Keep your leadership kind.

Because when you do, you don't just build a company —
you build a field of energy that lifts everyone it touches.

And that… is the real manifestation.

The universe expands through the work you do,
when you do it in alignment with who you truly are.

# From Me to You

When I began writing The Manifest Principles in Business, I didn't set out to write another book about leadership or growth.
I wanted to write about **energy** — the invisible current that moves through every team, every company, and every dream that's ever been built.

For years, I watched incredible people — creative, talented, driven — push themselves to exhaustion chasing success that never felt fulfilling. And I realized something I couldn't ignore:
we were taught how to manage business,
but not how to **be in energetic relationship** with it.

We were taught strategy without spirit.
Discipline without alignment.
Performance without purpose.

And yet… the companies that thrive — the ones that inspire, innovate, and magnetize opportunity — are the ones that operate in flow, not force. They don't just do business differently.
They vibrate differently.

That's what this book is about.

It's about remembering that business is not separate from energy, that leadership is not separate from soul,
and that abundance isn't something we earn — it's something we allow.

## Why I Wrote This

I've spent my life walking between two worlds —
the practical world of marketing, data, and growth strategies,
and the intuitive world of manifestation, energy, and higher guidance.

This book is where those two worlds finally shook hands.

It's proof that you can be ambitious and aligned.
That you can grow a business that's profitable and peaceful.
That you can build from trust instead of tension —
and still achieve more than you ever imagined.

It's not about abandoning strategy.
It's about elevating it.

When energy leads, everything else follows.

## A Gentle Invitation

If this book found you, it's because you're part of a new generation of
thought leaders —those who are ready to build from frequency first.

So take what resonates.
Integrate what aligns.
And trust that every time you return to stillness, the next right step will
reveal itself.

Let this book be a companion, not a conclusion.
Return to it when you forget, when you doubt, when you need to
remember who you are beneath the titles, the meetings, the deadlines,
and the noise.

Because at your core, you're not just leading a company —
you're leading energy.

And that's the most sacred leadership there is.

# Acknowledgments

Throughout my career, I've had the privilege of working for and alongside leaders who shaped not only my professional path but also my understanding of leadership itself. While not all have embraced the language of manifestation, each has played a profound role in helping me become who I am — reminding me that alignment, integrity, and courage show up in many forms.

**To Vrajesh Lal** — my first real boss and one of the earliest believers in my potential. Vrajesh taught me the art of taking bold chances, of trusting my instincts even when the path ahead wasn't clear. He led with quiet strength and unwavering integrity, always doing the right thing even when it wasn't the easy thing. Under his leadership, I learned that great leaders don't just give you opportunities — they see who you are before you fully do. His belief in me pushed me to stretch, to grow, and to step into every new challenge with both grit and grace.

**To Tim Costello and Melissa Morman** — for more than fifteen years, you created a space where I could grow beyond what I thought was possible. You led by example, building a culture of innovation, collaboration, and relentless curiosity. You encouraged me to think bigger, to lead with both head and heart, and to never stop learning. Working alongside you shaped how I see business — not just as a system of results, but as a living, breathing ecosystem of people, ideas, and purpose. The lessons I learned under your leadership continue to influence how I build, how I coach, and how I serve.

And to my family — **Alex, Kai, and Skyler** — thank you for grounding me, loving me, and cheering me on through every dream, late night, and creative storm. You are my greatest teachers in patience, perspective, and presence. Every word I write and every project I create is woven with the love, laughter, and life we share

**Christine Zanjanipour** is a creator, entrepreneur, and visionary voice in the world of conscious living and leadership. She is the founder of **Details Matter Books**, a boutique publishing imprint that celebrates intentional design, elevated storytelling, and the art of living with purpose.

The author of multiple lifestyle and personal growth works—including *The Manifest Principles*, *The Manifest Principles in Business*, *I Am Because I Say I Am*, *The Staring Game*, *The Hostess with the Mostest*, *Flourishing Bread Co.*, and *Yummers!*—Christine writes for those who believe that clarity, belief, alignment, and inspired action can transform not only lives, but entire organizations.

With over two decades of experience in **business development and data-driven marketing**, Christine has guided leading brands, coached high-performing teams, and helped companies bring consciousness into the workplace. Her unique approach blends strategic insight with the energetic power of manifestation—bridging the worlds of logic and intuition, data and energy, purpose and performance.

Beyond her books, Christine is the creative force behind several lifestyle ventures that reflect her passion for artistry, hospitality, and the joy of everyday beauty—from artisan bread and olive oil to elevated travel and mindful living.

She lives with her husband, **Alex**, along the Roaring Fork River in Glenwood Springs, Colorado, where the mountains inspire her to ski, bake, write, dream, and create experiences that remind others of what's possible when passion meets presence.

Christine believes in living deliberately, leading energetically, and noticing the beauty in every detail—because, in business and in life, **details always matter.**

# Let' Stay Connected

If you'd like to continue the conversation — through corporate workshops, manifestation coaching, or conscious business retreats — you can find me at:

Follow The Manifest Principles in Business

Instagram:
https://www.instagram.com/themanifestprinciplesinbusiness

Facebook:
https://www.facebook.com/themanifestprinciplesinbusiness

**www.DetailsMatterBooks.com**

I'd love to hear how this work moves through you and your company. Your stories, your insights, and your transformations keep this energy alive.

Because the more we share, the more we expand — together.

With clarity, belief, and a little bit of magic —